DOOLIN

People, Place & Culture

Eddie Stack

TINTAUN
GALWAY & SAN FRANCISCO

A paper based on 'The Storytellers' was presented at the
California Celtic Conference at UC Berkeley, California, March 2013.

An earlier version of 'The MacNamaras' was published in
I Sang in My Chains, annual journal of The Dylan Thomas Society
of Great Britain, 2003.

Muintir an Chláir Yearbook 2014, has an extract from 'The Way We Were'.

© Eddie Stack, 2016

ISBN 978-1-930579-03-3

Design: Bill Roarty, ES

Man Friday: Jamie MacDara Stack, Team Ballylara

Cover and frontis photographs by Michael Fitzgerald

Transportation: Ollie Liddy and Gerry Quinn

Published Worldwide by Tintaun, Galway & San Francisco

Many of the photographs in this book have come through
several hands over the years. In a few cases it was not
possible to identify or trace the photographers. We include
these photos in the spirit of goodwill towards Doolin,
her tradition-bearers and her people. If you know the
photographer or source from an unidentified photo,
send the information to info@tintaun.com and
we will update future editions of *Doolin*.

For Pakie Russell

◆

Folk Art is indeed the oldest of the aristocracies of thought...
it is the soil where all great art is rooted.

W.B. Yeats

◆

Acknowledgments

I'm grateful to all the Doolin tradition-bearers and informants who helped create this work—the Russell Brothers, the Killougherys, Paddy Pharaic Mhichil Shannon and the musicians, storytellers, singers and dancers who went before them and passed on their legacies. Special thanks to all in Doolin who gave me information, songs, stories, yarns, photos about the place and its heritage. To list names after so many years is difficult without failing to mention people, so thanks to you all.

Míle buíochas le Jackie Small, musicologist and P.J. Curtis, writer and broadcaster. Thanks to Eugene Lamb, Charlie Piggott, Tommy Peoples, Michael & P.J. Hynes, Kevin Griffin, Eoin O'Neill, Bríd and Seán Talty, Christy Barry, Dolores Keane, Andrew MacNamara, Jim Corry, Tara Connaghan, Terry Woods, Tony Reidy and Martin Hayes.

Thanks to Maureen Comber, Anthony Edwards, Carrie Stafford and the staff of Clare County Library and Local Studies Center for their help and support with the project. Thanks also to Siobhan Mulcahy, Bonzo, Phillip Morrison, Steve and Joe Wall, Jimmy Hill and Gerry Cleary. Thanks as well to Mick Moloney, Martin Breen, Michael Coady, Tom Liddy, John Fitzpatrick, Richard Gault, Michael Fitzgerald, Mary Gaynor, Gerry Mulkerrins, Pat Neary, Louis de Paor, Jane Kelton, John Caulfield and Ellen Murphy.

For library research help at National University of Ireland, Galway, thanks to Timothy Collins and Pauline Stack.

University College Dublin, National Folklore Collection: thanks to Patricia Moloney, MLIS; Criostóir MacCartaigh, archivist, and Professor Ríonach Uí hÓgáin, Director of the NFC, for permissions and access to materials.

At UC Berkeley, California: thanks to Tomás Walsh, Kathryn Klar, Dara Hellman, Dan Melia, Eve Sweetser, Gary Holland, Kathi Brosnan and all at the Celtic Studies Program.

In the book world, thanks to Vinnie Browne and all at Charlie Byrne's in Galway, Des Kenny in Galway, muintir Scéal Eile, Inis and all the indie booksellers who support my work. In the U.S., thanks to Alan Wherry, John Norton, Seán Heaney, Willy Vlautin and Peter Quinn. And the San Francisco production crew: Bill Roarty, Captain Midnight, Kay Burns and Lisa Zemelman.

Thanks to Mrs. Nora Canavan, Maria and Micheál and all at St. Catherine's for the hospitality. Buíochas le Clann de Staic—Aindrias, Éamon, Róisín agus Jamie MacDara; agus le m'uncail Seán Ó'Súilleabháin agus a chlann.

Finally, thanks to The Doolin Ferry Company and The Arts Council of Ireland for their help and support in bringing this book to fruition.

Doolin

TABLE OF CONTENTS

*

Introduction 6

People, Place & Culture 8

The Way We Were 48

The Music Makers 66

The Storytellers 119

The Gentry 137

*

Introduction

My earliest memory of Doolin is being by the little house over at the Ballaghaline pier with my father and his cousin Tim Murphy. Their aunt (Gertie Murphy) had lived there. I remember the wild sea and the wind. I was four or five years old and had never been as far away from my home in Ennistymon.

Jimmy Stack, my father, was well known in Doolin. He'd been at school with Gus O'Connor, Tim Flanagan and others, and spent his summer holidays at his aunt's house in Ballaghaline. He often said the happiest days of his life were when himself and Gus O'Connor played football on the road to the pier.

Our pub in Ennistymon was a regular stop for the Doolin people when they came to town or were passing through. Men drank porter in the bar and my mother served the women tea and sherry in the kitchen. They dropped in on their way to America and again when they returned home. No matter whether they were coming or going they were happy and brought a spark of light with them. Over the years I got to know Jack Garrihy, the Flanagans, Russells, Shannons, O'Connors, Guerins, O'Briens, Pakie Moloney and Michael Sherlock who used to cut turf with us, Jamsie Caoilte, John Long, Jimmy Danagher and many more.

One St. Patrick's Day I was in Doolin with my father and Jamo Reilly, fishing the Aille river, up from McDermott's in Roadford. We thought we could hear music, but dismissed it as the water warbling. Pakie Moloney came out the back door of the pub and waved at us. Fishing halted and as we went to him, the music got clearer, concertina and fiddle. We entered through the back door and into the dim bar. Pakie Russell and Paddy Killoughery played in the corner and a man danced with a sweeping brush in the middle of the floor. Hands were shook, two pints and a bottle of orange called. We stayed for hours and Kevin McDermott drove us home to Ennistymon, bicycles and all.

As orange juice gave way to porter, the fishing rod gave way to the mandolin and I spent more time in Doolin. There were fireside chats with Pakie Russell and tunes and stories in O'Connor's. Moonlight trips to Aran. Music sessions and porter sessions melded into one. On dry nights there would be visits to Paddy Pharaic Mhichil Shannon who lived in a cottage behind O'Connor's in Fisherstreet. Glimpses of a world gone by, slipping further and further away by the year. They gave hints of how Doolin evolved to what it is today.

In the early 1980s I began to jot bits and pieces down, and interviewed the remaining tradition-bearers. I had no plan in mind, just a curiosity as to why traditional arts survived so long in Doolin and why was it so different from anywhere else I knew.

On the way I learned about the older musicians and singers, dancing masters, house dances, Swaries, and Strawboys. Field notes from Séamus Ennis' visit after WWII, when he was collecting material for the Folklore Commission of Ireland, gave a snapshot of the music and singing in Doolin in the mid-1940s.

I learned that storytelling was an important Doolin folk art, and an often forgotten cultural jewel. From 1929 to 1945, Séamus Delargy of the Folklore Commission of Ireland recorded a collection of folktales in Irish which is one of the most important and largest in Western Europe. Delargy wrote that Doolin Irish was the purest he had ever heard and Doolin storyteller Stiofán Uí Ealaoire was the best he had ever come across.

At the opposite end of the social scale from tradition-bearers and the ordinary people were the Doolin gentry. They played a role in shaping the history of the area, from the MacClancys to the MacNamaras. Intelligentsia, black sheep, High Sheriffs and Members of Parliament, they left their mark and spread the name Doolin across Ireland and then Europe. They were all part of the Doolin matrix.

MANY YEARS LATER I've put these pages together, a few pieces of the jig-saw that is Doolin. I hope they give some depth and background to this special place and the people who make it so.

People, Place and Culture

Doolin is old country. A small coastal area in North West Clare, farmers, tradesmen and fishermen have lived here for thousands of years. They left their impressions on the landscape with standing stones, cromlechs, old forts, churches and castles. There are prehistoric kitchen middens here, a sign that some of the earliest shore dwellers in Ireland lived near Fisherstreet village. Early tradesmen had a stone-axe factory close by and their stone tools have been found in faraway Kerry and Galway.

Sandwiched between the Cliffs of Moher, the Burren and the Atlantic, Doolin has the magic of a place from another age. There's a theory that it was from around Doolin and the Burren that Tolkien got his inspiration for *Lord of the Rings*.[1] There's a happy, peaceful feeling here, timeless and unhurried. A patchwork of brown and green fields, good land and bad, roll down to the shore. It's criss-crossed by stone grey walls and wind-bent furze bushes. Out in the ocean, the Aran Islands are like turtles on the horizon. With the sharp dark Cliffs of Moher to the south and the grey-terraced Burren hills to the north, rain or shine, the scenery is spectacular. The Welsh artist Augustus John found Doolin a painter's paradise when he visited before the first world war on the invitation of Francis MacNamara.[2]

Landscape and history are important determinants of culture and it's little wonder that Doolin has a unique and rich culture and heritage. This spirit of Doolin comes through in the folklore, customs, music, song and stories of the generations that have lived here. The local tradition-bearers were people of remarkable character and ability, and provided the flux of social life until the last quarter of the 20th century. In this sanctuary to musicians, singers and dancers, the old Irish traditional arts and ways of life held out when they had faded elsewhere. This was the last outpost of the Irish language in Clare, and home to the last bastion of the great Irish storytellers.

Until the 1960s, Doolin was only visited by her near neighbours, the cognoscenti, and a coterie of British academics—mainly geologists, botanists, ornithologists and speleologists. By the mid-'70s it had become a stop on every hip backpacker's itinerary of Ireland. It all happened by word of mouth: first a trickle arrived, then a stream that became a flood. Doolin and her people unwittingly invented Irish cultural tourism. There were no signposts for the place back then and it wasn't on many maps. It was easier and quicker to get to the Aran Islands from Fisherstreet than it was to travel to the nearest market town, Ennistymon. Perhaps its remoteness ensured that the region had a longer Celtic Twilight than most other places. Nowadays Doolin is mentioned in every guidebook and travel map of Ireland. It is an essential stop for those who want to see the 'real Ireland' and every year tens of thousands journey there to hear music, meet the locals, enjoy the scenery, go to the Aran Islands and wonder at the Cliffs of Moher.

THE DISTRICT KNOWN as Doolin is made up of 46 small townlands, and its boundaries are those of the old Killilagh parish. The local place-names, most of which are in the Irish language, tell more than meets the eye about the area. Every field and stone has its story and place in time: *Cnoc an Chrochaire,* where survivors of the Spanish Armada were hanged in 1588 by the order of Boetius MacClancy; *An Lonn Dubh,* the reef that wrecked HMS Magpie in 1864; *Carraig na Loinge Buí,* a rock that a Connemara king brought across Galway Bay on a boat, long before history was written down.

In ancient times the district was known as *Tuath Clae,* 'the territory of Clae,' a statelet ruled by a sept of the O'Briens. Up to the Middle Ages most of it was held by the O'Connors and the MacClancys. The O'Connors had three castles—Doonagore, Ballinalacken and Doonmacfelim—and paid rents to the O'Briens of Thomond[3]. The MacClancys were rent-free because they were judges and Brehon lawyers for Thomond. They held Toomullin Castle and also a School of Law and Poetics at Knockfinn, near where the present day Catholic church stands. It was a prestigious school and attracted many scholars, establishing *Tuath Clae* as a stronghold of Brehon law and Irish poetry.

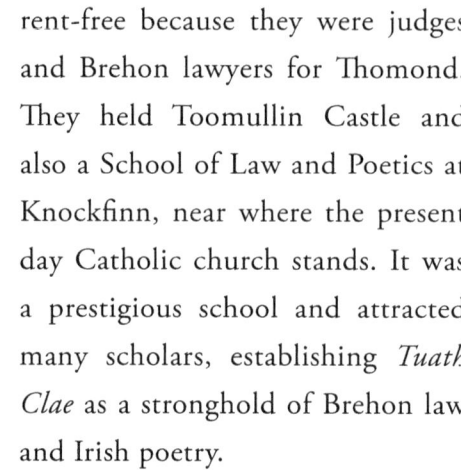

AN FEAR BRÉIGE
THE FALSE (ILLUSORY) MAN.
OUGHTDARRA, TUATH CLAE

In 1582, as English forces made headway into Clare, the O'Connors granted their lands to Turlough O'Brien of Ennistymon, hoping the arrangement would protect them against the encroaching armies of the Red Queen, Elizabeth. The deed was witnessed by Boetius MacClancy, who was rising to power and straying from his family's integrity. Boetius went on to become Doolin's blackest sheep and ended up owning most of *Tuath Clae* by hookery and crookery.

A FEW GENERATIONS after Boetius passed, Clare was devastated by the Cromwellian campaigns and the MacClancy families lost their lands. Famine and pestilence followed the wars, and the *Census of Clare, 1659*, recorded 186 Irish inhabitants in *Tuath Clae*, including one 'Sir Therlagh Magrath a poore decayed Bart'.[4] Most of *Tuath*

Townlands of Tuath Clae

Ardeamush: James' Height
Aughiska Mor: Big field of the water
Aughiska Beg: Small field of the water
Aughavinna: Field of the hill or field of the oath

Ballaghaline: Way to the islands
Ballinahuan: Place by the river
Ballynalacken: O'Loughlin's home
Ballycahan: O'Kane's home
Ballycullan: Place of little wood
Ballyryan: Ryan's home
Ballysallagh: Mucky place
Ballyvarna: Town on the top
Ballyvoe: Place of the cow
Boherboy: Yellow road

Caherkinalli (part of): Fort by the sea
Cahermaclancy: MacClancy's stone fort
Cahermacrusheen: MacRusheen's stone fort
Carnane: Small pile of stones
Cranagort East: Enclosure in tilled field (east)
Cranagort West: Enclosure in tilled field (west)
Carrowncleary: O'Cleary's Quarter
Cloghaun: Stepping-stones, causeway; old stone structure
Coogyulla: Province of the Ulstermen

Craggycordon East: O'Curridan's crag (east)
Craggycordon West: O'Curridan's crag (west)
Gortaclob: Field of the swallowhole

Doolin: (see sidebar, page 13)
Doonmacfelim: MacFelim's fort
Doonagore: Fort of the goats
Glasha Mor: Big stream
Glasha Beg: Small stream
Island: Island

Killilagh: Church of Aidhleach(?)
Knockacarn: Hill of the cairn
Knockagulla: Hill of the shoulder/hostage
Knocknaranahy: Fern hill
Lachtmurreda: Murreda's Flag
Lough North: Lake (north)
Lough South: Lake (south)
Lurrega: Long low ridge
Oughtdarra: Place of oak
Poulnagun: Hole of the hounds
Pouliskaboy: Hole of the yellow water
Teergoneen: Land without birds
Toumullin: District of the mill
Tournahooan: Black, or green, field of the cave

Clae was distributed to English adventurers and friendly Irish papists. By 1675 John Sarsfield owned the O'Connor castles of Doonagore and Doonmacfelim; John Gore had MacClancy's holdings at Toomullin and Knockfinn and Captain Hamilton had Ballinalacken. The old Doolin stock was dispossessed, and the new gentry in the parish all spoke English.

Known as 'good Irish Catholics' by the Crown, the Sarsfields came from Limerick and were granted substantial holdings around Doolin. Over time, the family became staunchly native, and, like their peers, the young Sarsfield males went to Europe and joined the Irish Brigade to fight for the French. While they were away at war, their sister Catherine married William MacNamara from up the coast and their fortunes changed. One of Doolin's most colourful and illustrious families had arrived, and after a few nervy years, William MacNamara gained ownership of the Sarsfield estate. The MacNamaras added to the holding bit by bit, and rivalled the Gores with their acreage and haughtiness.

BALLINALACKEN CASTLE: AN O'CONNOR STRONGHOLD UNTIL THE 17TH CENTURY

BY 1800 there were 300 'homes' in Doolin, sheltering a population estimated to be 2,000. They were mostly poor: tenant farmers, farm labourers, tradesmen and fisher folk; their language was Irish and their faith Catholic, with an underlay of pre-Christian beliefs, rituals and customs. Their year was dictated by the seasons and they had a close connection with the people of the Aran Islands, six miles out in the Atlantic. They wore homespun and woven woollens and linens. The women had red petticoats, short jackets and cloaks or shawls; the men wore hats and frieze breeches. Shoes were expensive and not part of everyday dress. They lived under British law, and an English traveller to the area noted:

*The genius and dispositions of the poorer class are in general good: they are amenable to the laws, to their superiors, and particularly to the magistrates. This appears to arise in a great measure from the kind and civilised manner in which the gentleman treats the peasant and the poor in this country.*5

The Irish Education Enquiry, 1824 lists three schools in Doolin.[6] All the schoolmasters were Catholics, with Oliver Davoren teaching at the new parish church in Knockfinn, built on the site of the old MacClancy School of Law and Poetics. The other two teachers, James Fitzpatrick and John Crean, taught in what were described as 'a wretched thatched shed' and 'a wretched hovel of the worst description' respectively. Davoren's school was the most popular and had a total of 100 pupils, while the others had about 40 each. No sacred scriptures were read or taught in any of the schools and they probably concentrated on the 3 R's—reading, writing and arithmetic.

DOOLIN ROSE a cut above its neighbours in 1830, when its own Major William Nugent MacNamara became Member of Parliament for Clare. A good man by all accounts, he was known as the 'poor man's magistrate'. Two years later a public house license was granted to Noreen Shannon of Fisherstreet, laying the foundation for O'Connor's Bar. By then Roadford and Fisherstreet were established villages. The gentry at the time were Mr. F. Gore, Esq. who lived in Aughavoher House near the sea at Ballaghaline, and Major W. N. Macnamara of Doolin House. English law was enforced by a coastguard station on Crab Island and constabulary barracks at Knockfinn.

The name Doolin

The district gets its name from the townland of Doolin, situated between the villages of Fisherstreet and Roadford. In the 1659 Census of Clare the townland is spelled Dowline and had a population of six. A mercurial property, it was owned by various illustrious gentry, including Boetius MacClancy, the Sarsfields and finally the MacNamaras. The 1787 Grand Jury Maps show Doolin House as the seat of power in the area. In the 1842 Ordnance Survey map of Killiliagh, the building is listed as Doolin Castle.

Of all the 46 townland names in *Tuath Clae*, there is some mystery as to where the name Doolin comes from. The Placenames Database of Ireland states: "Meaning unclear. Perhaps a compound of *dubh*, 'black' + *lann*, an obsolete Irish word meaning land." The Database gives the Irish version as *Dúlainn*. Notes from the Ordnance Survey Parish Namebook (1839), say 'meaning uncertain'. In The History and Topography of County Clare, James Frost writes Doolin may mean Dubh Linn, in Irish or "black pool", referring to the dark pools of the Aille River that flows through the villages.

Paddy Pharaic Mhichil Shannon thought that Doolin came from *An Dá Linn* or The Two Pools. He said there were two ponds in the field in front of Doolin House where children skated in the winters long ago. The pools were filled in after Doolin House was burned down in 1921.

TOWARDS THE END of the 1830s the district was surveyed by the Ordnance Survey Office. English engineers and sappers measured the land and Irish scholars came in their wake, jotting down notes, explanations and translations of old Gaelic words and names. The Ordnance Survey prepared the first accurate map of the area and did a listing of monuments. In 1839, Ordnance Survey Letters relating to the parish of Killilagh were written by John O'Donovan and Eugene Curry. They gave special mention to Toomullin Church, but the meaning of the name Killilagh remained elusive.

On the strength of the Ordnance Survey data, *The Parliamentary Gazetteer of Ireland*[7] of 1845 estimated the area of Tuath Clae as 12,357 acres, 1 rood, 15 perches, of which 22 acres, 2 roods, 12 perches were water. The population in 1841 was 2,047 and apart from the villages of Fisherstreet and Roadford, the parish had 8 hamlets. Regular attendance at the Catholic church was put at 400 and there were 62 Protestants in the area. There were four schools in the parish, one which was funded by the Baptist Society and two which closed during winter. The Baptist school had 74 boys in attendance and 8 girls. *The Gazetteer* does not provide numbers for the other schools.

Apart from those who could fish or afford fish, the diet was dependent mainly on potatoes, milk and butter. Work was scarce and employment for labourers was virtually non-existent from December until St. Patrick's Day. The month of July was known as *Hungry July,* because there was so little food before the potato harvest.

> Such is the distress of the labouring population in that part of the country, that no labourer is ever allowed now to take his potato crop off the ground until the rent is paid, or good security given for it. He never would be permitted to do so on his own responsibility.[8]

Ordnance Survey Letters by John O'Donovan and Eugene Curry, 1839

Parish of Killilagh[9]

In the Townland of Tuamullin in this Parish there is another Church of greater antiquity, measuring in length as it stands at present forty three feet and in breadth seventeen-feet, six-inches. Originally however, it was only thirty-three feet and four-inches in length for there was a small addition nine-feet and eight-inches built out of the west gable. The original west gable contained no feature but a small belfry placed on its top, but after the erection of the small addition or apartment just mentioned a pointed doorway was broken into it close to the south wall.

The original part of this Church had two doorways placed opposite each other, one in the north and the other in the south wall at the distance of two-feet from the original west gable, but they are now reduced to formless features (breaches). At the distance of five-feet from the east gable there is a round headed window at the height of four-feet from the ground outside and measuring on the inside six-feet by three-feet nine-inches and on the outside four-feet by five and a half-inches.

The east gable contains a neat window, wide and round on the inside and narrow and pointed on the outside. It measures on the inside seven-feet in height and three-feet eight-inches in width, and on the outside (where it is seven-feet from the present level of the ground) four-feet in height and seven-inches in width. The north wall is featureless. The modern apartment added to the west gable contains three windows, but they are too modern to merit particular description.

There is another small Church in the Townland of Oughtdara. In this Parish are three old Castles, one in the Townland of Doonagore which was lately repaired by Counsellor Gore from whose ancestors it is now erroneously supposed to have derived its name. This Castle is mentioned in the List of the Castles of Thomond preserved in Trinity College as belonging to Sir Donnell O'Brien. The second, in the Townland of Doon-Mac-Felim, which is mentioned in the aforesaid List as belonging to Tege Mac Murrogh (O'Brien) and the third in the Townland of Ballynalacken, which is mentioned in the List as belonging to the same Tege.

Besides the three Churches and three Castles already mentioned there are in this Parish the ruins of the more ancient dwellings of the Irish, as lioses and cahers. Of these there are several, viz:-

- A lios in Knockalassa, in the Townland of Aughiskabeg.
- A lios in Aughaveana Townland, after which it is called.
- Caher-reagh in the centre of a bog in the Townland of Cahercunnella.
- A fort in the Townland of Coogulla, called Tonwaun from the name of the subdivision of land on which it stands.
- A caher in the Townland of Caher MacClancy, which was the seat of the family of MacClancy, Brehons of Thomond.
- A caher in the Townland of Doon-MacFelim, generally called Caheradoon.
- There was a doon on the summit of a small green hill in the Townland of Doonagore, but it is completely effaced.
- A caher in the Townland of Glashabeg.
- A fort in the Townland of Glashamore.
- In the Townland of Cahermacrusheen there is a cromlech called by the usual name of Leaba Dhiarmada agus Ghraine.
- I find no other remain of the olden time in this Parish but the site of a sepulchral monument in the Townland of Laghtmurreda (Margarite's Monument) to which it has given name.

KILLILAGH CHURCH

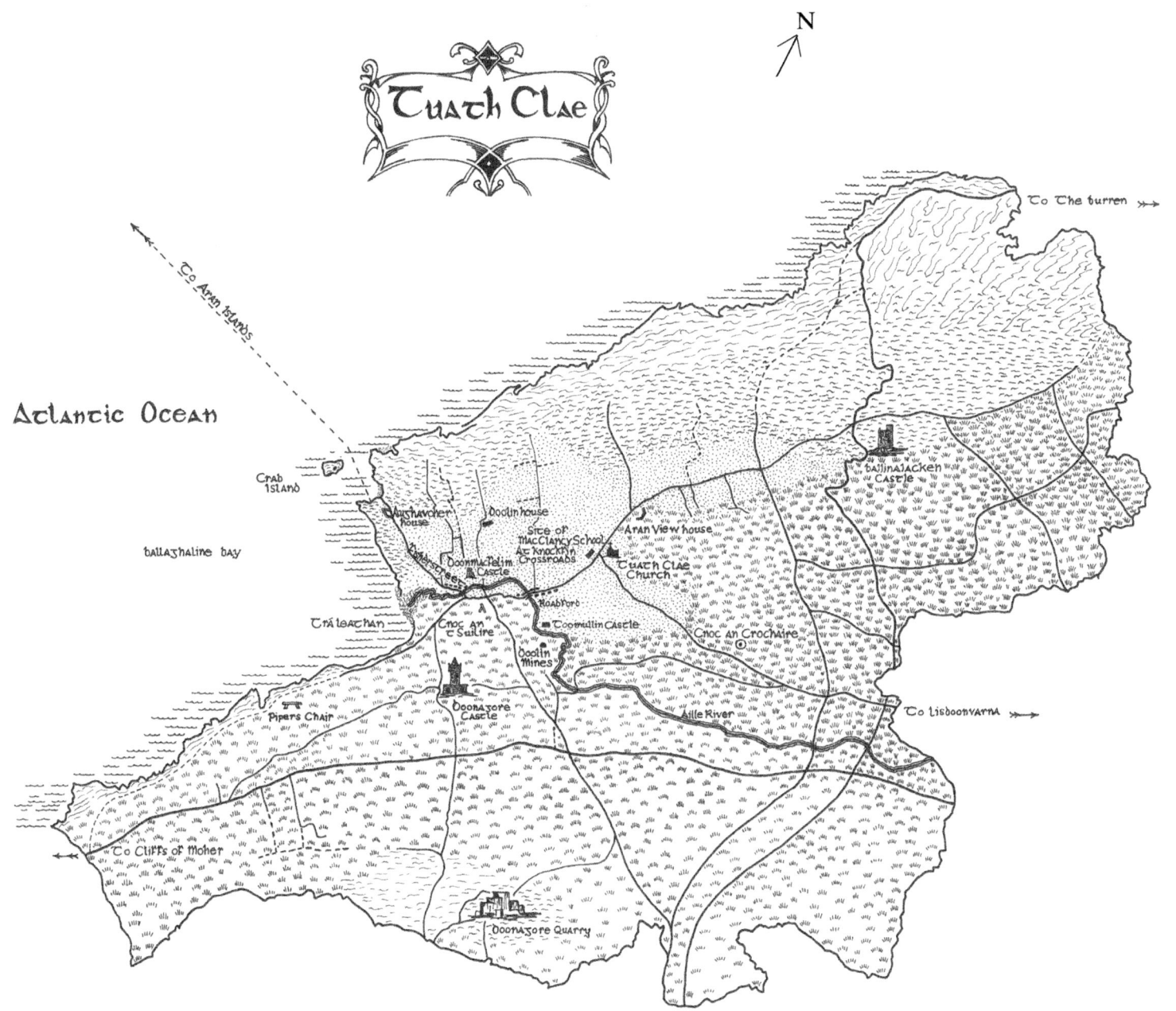

There was hardly a Doolin family unaffected by the Great Famine of 1845-48 and its aftermath. Poverty, starvation, disease, death and emigration wreaked havoc on the community. The times that followed were hard, a period which the old people called *an droch saol* or 'the bad life.' Doolin storyteller Stiofán Uí Ealaoire recalled:[10]

> In the times I saw growing up, poor people had no way of making a living. It was the hard life surely. There was very little flour, tea or sugar. They lived by the little bit of work they did themselves, sowed potatoes and a bit of wheat, and the ones that had no land to sow, they had to live on yellow meal. They had some butter and eggs, but very little meat or bacon, it wasn't around. The only time they had flour was at Christmas, a stone of flour and a couple of candles, that's the Christmas they had.
>
> There was a man who lived here in the hard times and he went to steal a turnip for his supper. 'Twas said the man who owned the garden stopped him and next morning neighbours found him dead in his cabin. I often heard my mother talk about it.
>
> There were no shops, but there were hucksters—old women who'd go to town and buy a couple of shillings worth of what was called *arán geal*, white bread. Then they'd go around the countryside selling bread to the housewives. The housewife might also buy an ounce of tea or a half-pound of sugar.
>
> We had to work hard from dark to dark. Big strong men who got work from a master got ten pence a day, a crown a week. He had to take care of a big family on that, maybe six or seven children. And he had to pay rent to the master so he could have a garden to sow potatoes for the year. Poor people had to pay big rents and if they weren't able, the landlord set the bailiff on them. If they had a cow the bailiff took it and they couldn't say a word. The following day they were on the side of the road and their cabin knocked down.
>
> "Go to the Workhouse or earn your living around Ireland!"
>
> The landlord would then rent out the piece of land to a man who was able to pay the rent. That's what made the big farmers around Ireland and forced others to take to the high seas when they weren't able to pay the rent.

According to the stories told by Stiofán Uí Ealaoire, Seán O'Carún (Johnny Carey), and others, many of the musicians around Doolin were pipers until after the Famine at least. Micho Russell said pipers from all over Ireland used to come on May Day to play at the Piper's

"Dead or gone to America"
Usual reply when someone asked where the occupants of ruined cottages were.

Chair near *Poll na nGall* in Luogh.

Stiofán told of a very good piper named Muirfí who lived in *Baile ui Choileáin*, near Doonagore. Muirfí had twelve sons and each of them played the pipes very well. To make a living they travelled around the country playing tunes and every so often they all returned home at the same time. On fine evenings, Muirfí and his twelve sons would gather on a hill near their house and the thirteen pipers would play the finest of tunes.

They were renowned for their playing of the slow air, "*Gol na mBan san Ár*"—The Women's Lament at the Slaughter. This epic piping piece simulates the march of the troops into battle, the struggle itself and the women lamenting the slain in the aftermath. Musicologist Brendan Breathnach said the piece relates to the victory of Lord Inchequin at Knockinnoss, County Cork, in 1647. The tune survived around Doolin until the late 20th century when Micho Russell played a version of it.

EMIGRATION was one of the legacies of the Famine, and most of the Doolin emigrants went to America. By the 1870s, there was an ongoing exodus from the area, encouraged by the letters and money sent home by those who had settled in the New World. The faraway country was attractive to the poor tenant farmers and labourers of Tuath Clae. At that time in America, a farm worker earned $35 a month, plus board and meals, and wages were double in spring and harvest. There was hope there and even the opportunity to own land: farmland in California could be bought for between $10 and $25 an acre.

Leaving became easier when the West Clare Railway began operating in July 1887. Now a train from Ennistymon or Lahinch could bring emigrants to the boat in Kilrush, Limerick or Dublin in a day, instead of several days by foot or carriage. With the railway, the number of visitors coming to North West Clare dramatically increased. The Victorian holiday-makers sojourned at Lahinch and Lisdoonvarna and usually viewed Doolin from a distance, as they travelled the coast road in horse-drawn carriages. Once in a while they ventured down through Fisherstreet and out to the sea at Ballaghaline. In 1891 a writer named H.B.H made the trip and wrote one of the first travel pieces about Doolin.[11]

> The drive from Lisdoonvarna to the Cliffs is a most enjoyable one, along the coast, with the Islands of Arran (sic) in view, and the ruins of another old telegraph-tower on the landscape, on the coast over Doolin; and here at this extreme west coast, down at the shore at Doolin is some of the best grazing land in the county, which is proverbial for its fattening quality. There is a tradition that an acre of this land fattens a bullock, and if its verdant appearance at all seasons of the year is any guarantee of richness, the land certainly must be prime. Ballaghaline is a fishing station, near Doolin, and being the nearest and most convenient place for visitors

staying at Lisdoonvarna, it is customary to hire a canoe for an excursion to the nearest of the Islands of Arran, which is about an hour's rowing from the mainland, with favourable wind.

The Arran people come here with fish to sell, and also to buy goods on the mainland. They bring cattle to neighbouring fairs and markets, and make purchases also, which they take back with them. Horses, cattle, and animals of every description are transported to and from the Island in open boats, and a cruel practice it is, owing to having no place but the beach to land and embark; the want of a harbour or quay of some sort is experienced by the fishermen themselves, who have no place to turn to for shelter when overtaken in a storm, while out at sea fishing. A breakwater connecting the mainland with Crab Island, a few hundred yards opposite the shore, would accomplish all that is necessary, and would be a great boon conferred on the poor men who have nothing to depend on except the 'harvest' which the sea produces for their support. The Government could not better employ the public money than in providing harbour accommodation for the fisherman of the mainland as well as for the Arran people who frequent Ballaghaline.

Driving from Lisdoonvarna to Doolin, subterranean passages may be observed, into which the streams flow, and are carried underground to the sea beyond, and near the coast are openings which indicate where these subterranean chambers exist.

According to *Guy's Directory, 1893,* Doolin had an emigration agent, Mr. Michael Flanagan who helped arrange passage to America, Canada and Australia. The directory lists twelve shopkeepers and vintners in the parish and two national schools. Robert Johnstone of Aran View was Justice of the Peace and there were eight large farmers or 'ranchers', as well as landlords MacNamara and Gore. The other families who worked the land were tenant farmers. At that time, Irish was still the spoken language amongst the locals, though English was the language of commerce and most of the young had some knowledge of it. The area was recovering from the famine and had a thriving fishing industry. Fish were salted and cured, and sold to dealers who brought them down to Ennistymon in barrels. These were loaded on the train, and sent to Limerick, Dublin and further afield.

The last decades of the 19th century saw an Irish renaissance, as interest in Irish culture and heritage became widespread. During this time, Thomas Johnston Westropp carried out archaeological studies around Doolin, examining and mapping old cahers, castles, forts and monuments. Westropp was an engineer by profession, and his work was more detailed than that done by the Ordnance Surveyors in 1839. He said of their efforts:

> The Ordnance Maps, both of 1839 and of the most recent survey, are, I regret to say, most deficient in the marking of the natural features and antiquities of these townlands. The formal contour lines are misleading …important forts are unmarked and one name is attached to a wrong fort. It is much to be regretted that no one seems to have collected any descriptions of the forts of this most interesting county till 1839: and then the writers of the Ordnance Survey letters lost an unrivalled opportunity.[12]

Westropp was impressed by Doolin's antiquities, and the stories and legends, superstitions and beliefs that he heard from the local people fascinated him. Westropp and his friends from the Limerick Field Club made excursions to Doolin and were probably the first day-trippers to the place. On an outing in July 1899, they found evidence of an old stone axe factory in the sand dunes near Fisherstreet as well as kitchen middens that indicated people have been around there for at least 4,500 years.[13]

Doolin

Thomas Westropp visited the castle ruins in May, 1878 and later wrote:

> It is about 46-feet high and has four stories, being 29-feet in external diameter, and 12-feet inside on the ground level; the walls are 8-feet and 6-inches thick. The door faces east and was recessed and chamfered. We find traces of bar holes and three recessed partly built up, one being a window. A staircase from the south jamb of the door rises through the thickness of the wall.
>
> The upper wall is much split and decayed, and the battlements are entirely removed. The tower had a bawn, a strong walled enclosure to the north, much of which was standing in 1878.

Doolin icon Doonagore Castle is one of only three round castles in County Clare. Built by the O'Connors in the fourteenth century, it later passed on to the O'Briens and then to Boetius MacClancy. Local folklore says it was in Doonagore Castle that Boetius sentenced the survivors of the Spanish Armada to death in 1588. Built with flagstone from *Trá Leathan*, the castle gets its name from 'fort of the goats' or 'fort of the small hills.'

When the dust settled after the Cromwellian campaigns, the Sarsfields took possession of Doonagore Castle from the MacClancys. Subsequently it belonged to the Gores, who fabricated a history that claimed it was called after them. The Gores let it fall into ruin over the centuries. Doonagore Castle was restored in the 1970s by Irish-American tobacco tycoon John O'Gorman.

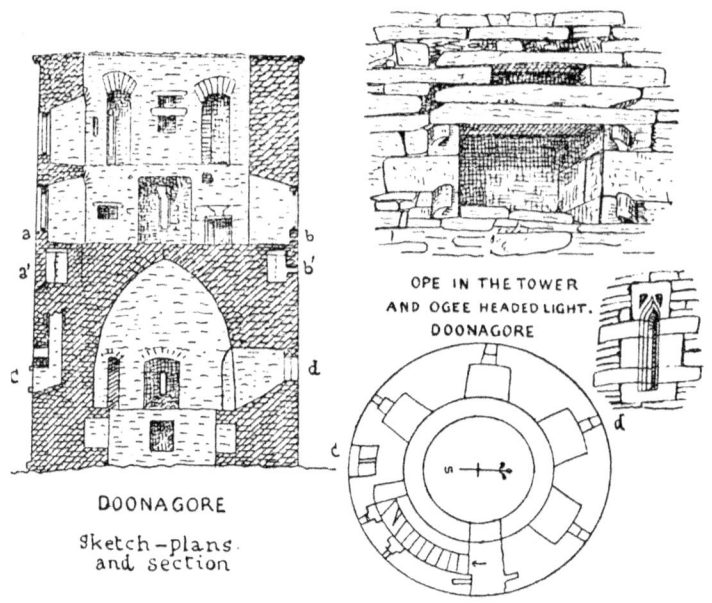

Drawing by Thomas Westropp, 1878

Doonagore Village, 1900s

SINCE THE TIME of the stone axe factory, stone played an integral part in Doolin life. It was a natural resource and the area bred quarry men, stone cutters and stonemasons. It produced its own vernacular architecture, walls of flat olive-brown stones laid with tight joints, smooth flagstones for roof and floors: a great defence against the winter winds that blow in from the Atlantic. Stone was a life-saver again to the area at the end of the nineteenth century, when quarries opened at Doonagore, Luogh and Caharbarnagh.

This was the first major industry in North West Clare, and brought huge employment to the area. Doonagore[14] was a major operation, run by a British company owned by George Watson. He built Doonagore Village Street to house his staff and at one point it had a post office, shops, possibly a sheebeen and the first telephone in the area.

Doonagore quarry covered 30 acres with three work faces. Both roofing slate and flagstone were quarried and Watson constructed over three miles of a narrow-gauge railway to take the flags from the quarry by steam engine. Flags were then transported down to Liscannor for export. At first the stone was brought down by horse and cart, but later steam trucks took the loads down to the quay. Flags from Clare were shipped out to pave the streets of England and the floors of the Royal Mint in London. Watson advertised Doonagore stone as *Shamrock Stone*, described as having a *Beautiful French-grey colour for Architectural Work*.

Quarrying work was hard and dangerous and the pay was only a few shillings a day. At one time, over 500 local men worked the quarries, many of them cutters and stone dressers. The 1901 census also lists several people from outside the area working in the quarries. The management and technical staff were mostly British, but there were labourers from all over Ireland who lodged locally and helped the economy.

Blasting at Doonagore quarry is thought to be responsible for the Bog Slide of 1900. It happened on a Sunday in October when most people were at Mass. The bog slipped in Luogh and rushed down the slope towards the sea. Two people were killed as it swept all before it, in a wave that some said was thirty-feet high. The bog avalanched into the ocean, where it floated like an island until a storm broke it up some weeks later. Micho Russell said there was a hen house and a hen on the bog-island, and two men from Fisherstreet went out in a curragh and rescued the fowl.

Doonagore flags beinged loaded for export at Liscannor, early 1900s

Doolin went into the annals of the revolution in September 1908, when tenant farmers drove the cattle from the lands of big ranchers, as far as Ennistymon and into the grounds of Ennistymon House (now the Falls Hotel), which was then the home of Doolin landlord and High Sheriff of Clare, H.V. MacNamara. The incident is recalled in song and story as the Doolin Cattle Drive.

Over 40 men were arrested for the action and brought to court in Ennistymon two weeks later. On court day, Ennistymon was black with people from all over the county, who came to support the Doolin men. Over 400 policemen were drafted into the town, and they lined the streets with batons drawn. When the verdict was announced and the Doolin drivers sentenced to jail, a riot broke out. The police baton-charged the crowd, but they fought back, injuring several policemen. The incident marked a turning point in North Clare history, as power passed to the people and green banners were unfurled in Ennistymon. The day was remembered locally as *Lá an Bhaton Charge*.

A few years later the first bohemians came to Doolin, at the invitation of Francis, the eldest son of H.V. MacNamara. The painter Augustus John visited, as did George Bernard Shaw and members of the Bloomsbury Set. They were the first of the 'arty' crowd to arrive, and spent some heady summers around Doolin in the early years of World War I. The earliest reference to music and craic in a Doolin pub comes from Augustus John, who wrote in *Chiaroscuro*: "He (Francis) would often take me down to the little sheebeen (sic) in

Francis MacNamara's friends, The Westropps on Doolin Beach, 1914

Fisherstreet, to watch the dancing and listen to Irish sagas and songs."[15]

WHEN THE WORKERS at the stone quarries went on strike for better pay and conditions in 1914, the company decided to close down. A British boss addressed the workers in Doonagore and his speech was met with cold silence. He asked if any of the workers wished to say anything and a man named Jerome Connole indicated he did. In typical Doolin fashion, Connole said, "I'd like to sing a song."

He sang 'In Our Own Dear Land', which Micho Russell later learned from him and preserved.

DOONAGORE: AFTER THE GOLDRUSH

In Our Own Dear Land

Chorus
Boys, oh boys, I'm glad to meet you,
If I'd money, trath I'd treat you.
'Tis with a song I'd fondly greet you
In our own dear land.

Do your best for one another,
Love your neighbor as your brother,
Party feelings we must smother
In our own dear land.

Chorus

Now in this age of agitation,
While we seek Home legislation
We're not in need of separation
To ruin our own dear land.

Chorus

The British commons they must own
But they have plenty business of their own
So let us settle ours at home
In our own dear land.

WITH THE WINDING down of the quarries, hundreds of men were left unemployed and destined to emigration or the trenches of WWI. It was a severe blow to the area and another drain on the population. Much of the emigration was to America, and as men went, women followed. The only upside was the amount of going-away parties and the house dances that went with them. The area was still predominately Irish speaking, but almost all the young people had English.

Doolin stepped briefly on to the international stage in August 1918 when a German submarine brought Thomas Dowling, a member of Roger Casement's brigade, close to shore. In the dark, he mistook Crab Island for the mainland and landed there, destroyed his rubber dingy and then discovered that he was trapped. In the early morning he was rescued by Doolin fishermen Tom Lynch and the Davenport brothers, who brought him to Ballaghaline. Later that day he was arrested near Ennistymon in what Pakie Russell wryly called 'an event which changed the course of the First World War.' Lynch and the Davenports were brought over to London to give evidence at Dowling's trial for treason. He was sentenced to life in jail but got out in six years.

Doolin was relatively unscathed by the War of Independence. H.V. MacNamara was winged in the arm by an IRA bullet in 1919 but survived. His son Francis sided openly with Sinn Féin and that caused a rift between them. Doolin House was razed to the ground at the end of the war, a casualty of the struggle.

BRITISH SOLDIERS TAKING A BREAK OUTSIDE AUGHAVOHER HOUSE, THE GORE SUMMER RESIDENCE NEAR BALLAGHALINE, 1919

ROADFORD VILLAGE, circa 1900

BEFORE THE FOLKLORE of Ireland Society was set up in Dublin, there were very few stories in the Irish language from Clare. Intuiting that the Doolin area held stories and storytellers, Séamus Delargy from the Society arrived there on August 3rd, 1929. He took lodgings with the Carey family in Luogh and it was a fortuitous choice. Johnny Carey was a storyteller and Delargy said,

> I could not have got a better lodging for to this house came all the storytellers, singers and musicians for miles around.[16]

At that time, the Irish-speaking population in Doolin was dwindling and Delargy knew he was an 11th-hour chronicler racing against time. Over six years, he recorded nearly 500 stories, hundreds of seanachas pieces, proverbs and vocabulary. It is an astonishing oral library, revealing a hidden Doolin jewel. He was the first to record and document Doolin Irish, which he said had few rivals for richness and purity. His biggest discovery was Stiofán Uí Ealaoire, from whom he recorded 150 tales, probably the greatest collection of stories collected from a single source in Western Europe. The Folklore Society appointed a local collector to the area and Seán MacMathúna continued Delargy's work around Doolin, collecting the equivalent of 10,000 foolscap pages of stories, folklore and traditions in the course of his life.

Delargy was a well-known scholar internationally, and had many contacts with American universities. He was instrumental in the selection of Luogh for inclusion in a research programme undertaken in Ireland known as the 'Harvard Irish Survey' (1931-1936). Luogh was an area where most of the older people still spoke Irish and it was still largely steeped in tradition, yet not untouched by modernity. This was an era of the house dances and card tournaments, vanishing ways of life and high emigration. Two doctoral students in anthropology at Harvard University, Conrad M. Arensberg and Solon T. Kimball, undertook the fieldwork. Like Delargy, the researchers lodged with the Carey family in Luogh. Their study was published as "Family and Community in Ireland"[17] and is a classic snapshot of a society in transition. Arensberg wrote "The Irish Countryman," some of which deals with customs, beliefs and the way-of-life of the Doolin people in the 1930s. Their work broke away from empirical anthropological study and garnered much interest at the time. Years later, it was through Arensberg and Kimball that the photographer Dorothea Lange came to Clare with her camera for Life magazine.

The 1930s were bleak, apart from the house dances and American Wakes, which had the Doolin musicians going seven nights a week. The earliest evidence of music being played in the area only came to light in 1935 with the identification of a bronze harp peg, which had been found years earlier by a man digging a potato garden near the walls of the old church in Toomullin.[18] The peg was in very fine condition and the National Museum dated it from sometime between the 8th and 13th century.

Between 1937 and 1938, local schoolchildren took part in a national project now known as the Schools' Manuscript Collection. It was a revolutionary scheme in which the children were encouraged to collect and document folklore and local history, customs, beliefs, and work practices from local elders. The Doolin school children collected valuable material of a vanishing way of life in the district. The following was collected from Seán Pól Ó Flanagáin:

My Own District

My name is Seán Pól Ó' Flanagáin. I live in the townland of Carnane, in the parish of Tuath Clae, in the Barony of Corcomroe. There are eleven thatched houses and two houses with slate roofs in Carnane. It got its name from a big mound of stones that were here long ago.

There are nine people over the age of seventy years in Carnane and they all speak Irish. The old people are: Máire Ní Flanagáin, Maitias Ó' Flanagáin, Mícheál Ó' Flanagáin, Seán de Róiste, Mícheál Ó' Concubhair, Nóra Ní Concubhair, Tomás de Scéalas, Liam de Scéalas agus Bríghid de Scéalas.

There are a lot of bogs in the parish.

WHILE THE SCHOOLCHILDREN were collecting folklore, Doolin hit the motherlode in 1937, when Judge Michael Cummins from Ballyvaughan opened a phosphate mine at Toomullin, near the Aille River in Roadford. It was an open-cast mine and the enterprise grew with the outbreak of the Second World War, as foreign phosphate could not be imported. To satisfy demand, the government opened an underground mine on the other side of the river in 1941 and Doolin was booming.

That year, while Judge Cummins' company was digging a channel to divert the river, a number of important ancient items were found near St. Brecen's old church in Toomullin. They included a stone ring, two boar's tusks, a copper coin and a zoomorphic brooch, found in a layer of yellow clay, about six-feet below the surface. Judge Cummins presented the find to the National Museum, which estimated the ring was from the early Christian era and the brooch was possibly even older. The coin was undecipherable and probably from a much later date.[19]

The mines brought electricity to the parish and at one stage 600 men worked in the mines, while lorries ferried phosphate non-stop to Cork and Dublin for processing. Conditions were dirty and unhealthy, with lots of dust and smoke in the tunnels. The work could be dangerous and there were tragic accidents. Surface men were paid £2 for a five-and-a-half day week; underground workers got £2-11-0. The mines brought prosperity to the area and softened the hardship of the war years. Musicians recalled that time as being 'hectic' with the amount of house dances happening locally.

THE IRISH TOURIST ASSOCIATION came to Doolin during its 1930s survey of Ireland's beauty spots and holiday places. The ITA wrote:

> From Doonagore to the sea there is a steep incline and a mile further north there is an abrupt change from rank grass and heather to the lush fattening lands at Doolin, said to be the most fertile plain in Ireland. About a mile to the west of Doolin (Fisherstreet) is Ballaghaline, a famous bathing centre, where grand diving facilities are available off the pier. Boating and fishing facilities are also afforded.[20]

DURING THE WAR YEARS, Doolin beach at Ballaghaline became a popular seaside destination of visitors to nearby Lisdoonvarna. Gertie Murphy lived in a small cottage near the pier. A trained nurse and traditional healer, she served tea and homemade scones to visitors. This was the first facility in Doolin to cater specifically to visitors. On Sunday afternoons, a few musicians gathered at a concrete patio beside her house and played for dancers.

The high point of the wartime summer was the Doolin gala day, held at Ballaghaline. A regatta of sorts, it featured swimming competitions, curragh racing, climbing the greasy pole and other challenges. A number of sideshows including Wacker Daly's *Wheel of Fortune* and his wife's roulette table added to the excitement.

THE DOOLIN MINERS, 1942

Front row (l-r): Player Flaherty, Gus Murray, Paddy Linnane, Jackie Fitzpatrick, Willie Driscoll, Michael Moloney, Austin Davenport, Corkus O Loughlin, John Lynch. **2nd row:** Mattie Doherty, Jamesie Woods, Paul Darcy, Kazer Guerin, Packie Kelly, Landen Timmy {Shannon}, Tommy Killoughry, Mattie Sean Ryan, Barber Styke (O Donoghue), Gus O Connor. **Back row:** Micho Russell. Peter Moloney, Pap Donoghue, Mick O Connor, Jacko Shannon, Gusie Linnane, Michael O Loughlin, Danno Scales, Michael Egan. Tomas Shannon, Thomas Williams.

A FEW DAYS after World War II finished, in September 1945, musician and folklore collector Séamus Ennis came to Doolin for the first time. He was working for the Folklore Commission and journeyed there on the instruction of Séamus Delargy. He arrived by bicycle and got lodgings with Gertie Murphy in Ballaghaline. By that time the area was almost all English-speaking and storytelling sessions were seldom; the social flux at gatherings was now music, song and dance. Ennis quickly befriended the local 'king', Cuckoo (Pat) O'Brien. Ennis said that Cuckoo "spoke fine Irish and I spent the afternoon talking to him. His father had songs, he said, but he never learned them."[21]

Ennis described Cuckoo as a 'lifesaver' who watched over swimmers from his curragh, in case they got into difficulties. Ennis counted twenty horse-drawn sidecars, four people in each, stopping by the beach one evening.

It was a beneficial visit for the young collector and he met the young Pakie Russell and Peaitsín Flanagan, and collected the song '*Mairnéalach Loinge Mé*' from 'Styke' Donoghue. The following extract from his diaries describes his first encounter with Styke and later a grand night at the home of Anthony Moloney, near the bridge at Fisherstreet.

GERTIE MURPHY, 1895

Friday, September 28

I spent the afternoon with Peaitsín Ó' Flanagáin. I wrote a religious version of the words of 'Seán Mac Duibhir an Ghleanna' ['Seán Mac Duibahir of the Glen'] from him that I had not heard previously. And afterwards we went down to Ó Maoldhomhnaigh's house, where a number of local people had gathered listening to old people and talking and discussing matters.

Styke' came—Micheál Ó Donnacha (c.70) from a house down below. Yes indeed I omitted to mention a previous occurrence.

As I was coming up at six o'clock or so I saw a small man walking along the road ahead of me and he was carrying a bucket of milk or water. As I caught up with him—and I know he was aware that I was the person who was approaching—he appeared to sing softly to himself. And when I caught up with him, I recognised 'Cailín Deas Crúite na mBó' ['The Pretty Girl Milking her Cow'] without any words.

"Good day," he said to me, "Isn't it a fine evening?"

"It is indeed, thanks be to God," I said, "and that was a lovely tune you had just now."

"It is an old one I heard the old people sing long ago," he said, as if he did not care, and clearly he was enjoying himself.

We had only a short distance to go when we arrived at his house, and he told me to go to Ó' Maoldhomhnaigh's house later. I said I would go. That was 'Styke.'

Yes, Peaitsín and myself were not long in the house, smoking tobacco and talking when 'Styke' walked in. He was introduced to me and went to smoke his pipe, and Peaitsín sang some song (that he had learned from a book) and shortly afterwards 'Styke' sang 'Mairnéalach Loinge Mé' ['I Am a Ship's Sailor'] and I wrote it down from him. I had to sing a song for every song they sang, and a pleasant night ensued, with songs and amusing stories from both Peaitsín and Micheál ('Styke.')

A young man took a tin whistle from his pocket and played some tunes for us, and I had to play some tunes then after that. It was quite late when Styke remembered old tunes and accompanying verses and I wrote them down from him. I had to promise both of them the words of 'Chailín Deas Crúite na mBó' ['The Pretty Girl Milking her Cow']. I sent them from Dublin at a later date.

That night was the most enjoyable night I have ever spent, thanks to the Moloney family, Peaitsín and Micheál Ó' Donnacha, who had given so generously of their material at the fireside, as their forebearers had done previously.

WITH THE END of the war, imported phosphate was available again and mining in Doolin was no longer viable. Workers protested en masse, but Eamon de Valera, who was their public representative at the time, said it was uneconomical to keep the mines open because it was cheaper to import phosphate from segregated South Africa.

The closing of the mines was a blow to the area and emigration resumed. Dark and dreary years followed, brightened annually by the gala-day at Ballaghaline and the Doolin Greyhound Coursing Meeting. People gathered for these events, got merry, played music, sang and danced.

English geologists who had been exploring the caves around Doolin before the war returned in the late 40s. They became a familiar summer sight appearing out of the ground like black rabbits and having a few bottles of beer in local pubs after a day underground. Known as The Potholers, they were mostly university academics, and members of English caving clubs.

In 1952 the Craven Pothole Club discovered the Pol-an-Ionain cave in the townland of Craggycordon.[22] The cave is 1,400 feet in length and contains the largest chamber by far of all the caves in North West Clare. It also contains one of the largest stalactites in Europe, hanging from the roof of The Great Chamber. Known as Doolin Cave, the site is now a major tourist attraction.

THE GREAT CHAMBER, POL AN IONAIN

In 1953 the potholers discovered an open cave passing under the Aille River. One of the potholers, D.A.S. Robertson, composed *The Ballad of the Doolin Cave* about the discovery, sung to the air of 'The Rio Grande.' It's interesting that they realised that theories have no place in Doolin.

Expect the unexpected.

The river that's known as the Aille
Adown near Doolin
It's this we go under, oh, ever so dryly
'Way down in the Doolin Cave.
So 'way theories away,
away from Doolin,
Exploded are theories
Except where the beer is
Kept down at Lafferty's bar.

Lafferty's Bar, Roadford

Located where present-day McGann's is, near the bridge in Roadford, Lafferty's was probably the quietest bar in Doolin. It was the haunt of a local man called Lipton who lived under the bridge in the dry season, and the potholers' custom must have been a welcome weight to the cash box. Across the river was Considine's bar (now McDermott's), which was also a grocery shop and post office. The Doolin mines were behind Considine's in Toomullin. In Fisherstreet, O'Connor's was also a pub and grocery shop.

Doolin was largely a community of small farms in the 1950s. Houses were mostly single-story thatched or slated cottages. Blue and green fishnets tied down thatch and turf against the west wind and round, glass floats decorated gate piers. The only tourists were the aforementioned English cavers who came for a few weeks during the summer. There was no employment and emigration was steady. There were few cars and even the number of visitors who used to come to the beach from Lisdoonvarna declined. When Gertie Murphy died, the tea house at the pier closed down and the Sunday music session ended. There was little or no music in the pubs and not much business either. Bleak years.

Séamus Ennis had livened things up a bit when he returned to Doolin in 1949, to record material for his *Radio Éireann* programme. This was the first time Doolin tradition-bearers were broadcast, including Micho and Pakie Russell and Paddy Killoughery. Séamus came back to record the musicians for the BBC's '*As I Roved Out.*' Ciarán MacMahúna brightened things further when he came to get music for his Radio Éireann programmes '*Ceolta Tíre*' and '*Job of Journeywork*'. As well as the Russells and Paddy Killoughery, Ciarán recorded Martin 'Tarbert' Killoughery lilting and playing concertina.

In the mid 1950s, Gus O'Connor had a traveling shop that went around the parish a few times a week, selling groceries and the odd bottle of porter to customers. At night he served behind the bar and discussed the affairs of the world with locals Jamsie and Martin Caoilte, Bobby Guerin, Landen Shannon and others. Time passed slowly, but the conversation and banter was always good. There was music and song on only two nights of the year—in October after the annual greyhound coursing, when Pakie Russell and Paddy Killoughery played for winners and losers alike, and on Christmas Eve, a very late night sing-song with Dean Hynes, the Davoran brothers and other old-timers, many who sang in Irish.

O'Connor's was the nearest pub to the Aran Islands and the first and last port of call for the islanders when they visited the mainland. Sometimes there was as much Irish as English spoken in O'Connor's. Always a pub with a convivial atmosphere conducive to merriment, it was here music collectors and radio people resorted when they came to record the Doolin tradition-bearers. The Russell brothers from the townland of Luogh were in their prime then. Concertina, flute and whistles, Pakie, Micho and Gusie, had a hearty, simple style of playing and a huge collection of tunes native to the area. They were the sound of Doolin and they would change the fate and fortune of the region.

Gus O'Connor believed that the change began on the August Holiday weekend of 1959, when the Clare County Fleadh Cheol was held in Lisdoonvarna. It was scorching hot weather and the Fleadh was choc-a-bloc with people, ice-cream vendors, roulette tables, trick o' the loops and chip-vans. Pubs were packed and there was little comfort in drinking or listening to music.

Pakie Russell was unsuccessful in the senior concertina competition and headed out to O'Connor's for solace. He had hardly landed there when Séamus Ennis, Willie Clancy, Martín Byrnes, Martin Talty, Leo Rowsome, Ciarán MacMathúna and a small group of friends arrived from Lisdoonvarna. The music session that followed is said to have lasted all night and well into the following day. By then news of it had attracted a few more car loads from Lisdoonvarna. Word spread that Doolin was a special place for music, and all that went with it.

JOHN O'CONNOR WITH FRIENDS AND CUSTOMERS, 1955

WHEN DOOLIN musicians travelled to fleadhs outside the county, they met kindred spirits and invited them to visit some time. By the early '60s a sprinkling of Irish musicians and music lovers began coming to Doolin for the weekends. Visitors were welcomed with the proverbial open arms. In the days before the 'bed and breakfast', they slept on couches, settle beds, in hay sheds or camped in back gardens. Still remote and almost untouched by the outside, Doolin people had a different world view. More pagan than papist, they were a happy community and warmed to visitors who appreciated their values. And being far off the beaten track in those years, pub opening hours were lax and often when the bars closed, there were parties—sessions in local houses that lasted till dawn. Jamsie Caoilte frequently played host at his cottage down near the bridge in Fisherstreet and Rory O'Connor sometimes brought the select and the anointed to his place up in Doonagore. There were tunes, songs, stories dancing and other 'performance art.' Occasionally there was a lot of *poitín*.

Roadford pubs were somewhat under the radar in those days, but McDermott's (Considine's) was a 'secret haunt' of Pakie Russell and Paddy Killoughery. It was here the poet Michael Coady met Pakie when he dropped into the pub for a pint one summer's afternoon in 1963.

On Saturday nights there was set dancing in McDermott's, often livened up by Tim Flanagan, Jim Reidy and their friends who drove up from Ennis for the fun. Tim was a well-liked local man who inherited Lafferty's pub and set about renovating it in the late '60s. The pub was a healthy addition to the scene and was another venue for good local sessions. The enterprise got too big for Tim and he sold the pub. It eventually became McGann's.

When the 1960s' 'Ballad Boom/Folk Revival' kicked in, Doolin was established as the place to hear real traditional Irish music, have the *craic* and be part of a living culture. The fun, banter, tunes and stories—the once vital elements of the old country house gatherings—were somehow rekindled in Doolin pubs. More and more came to the place and a few bed and breakfasts opened.

Back then, Doolin was seasonal—fairly busy on the long summer weekends and easy-going during the week. In the pubs at night, locals outnumbered visitors by far, and sometimes there were no visitors at all. There was music in O'Connor's most nights, and on a good night sets were danced and songs aired. As the '60s peaked, folkies and hippies from abroad discovered Doolin. Writing about O'Connor's and the influx of visitors, Michael Coady noted:

> Backpackers from all over the world were amazed and delighted to find...a place where 'real' folk musicians played music which was a living thing and not something dead for centuries and artificially resurrected by scholarly types who met in very self-conscious folk-clubs at weekends.[23]

FISHERSTREET, EARLY 1960S

Many were American and European students, others were drop-outs seeking peace, love and music. These young men and women gave a further sparkle to the music sessions and craic in the pub. Locals who came of age during this time were blessed by the world coming to their doors.

In the meantime, Micho Russell found fame in late middle age and began to travel to Dublin and London, captivating audiences with his droll way of being and his pure Doolin music. Micho enticed more people to visit and Gus O'Connor renovated his pub to make room for them.

By the 1970s, Doolin was known beyond Ireland. A French film crew arrived in 1973 and captured a rare music session with piper Willie Clancy, Tony MacMahon and fiddler Seamus Connoly joining the local musicians.[24] It is a

MICHO RUSSELL AND PADDY KILLOUGHERY

Sometimes islanders came in on the last crossing, an occasion often marked with an after-pub party. One at Bill O'Brien's caravan in Ballaghaline is immortalised in a poem by Knute Skinner.

quintessential old Doolin session and captures the magic of the time and sense of the place. It was a big night, a meeting of the princes of Clare music. A night when Doolin was 'cooking' and there was magic in O'Connor's.

IN SUMMER 1970, Bill O'Brien bought a curragh from Rory O'Connor for £40 and launched the first ferry service between Doolin and Inisheer, the nearest of the Aran Islands. The fare was ten shillings return and locals and islanders travelled free. The service soon became another reason to come to Doolin and the following year, O'Brien bought a fiberglass boat which carried more passengers.

Paddy Pharaic Mhichil Shannon and Jamsie Caoilte, were frequent travelers, as were Gussie Russell and Rory O'Connor. The ferry strengthened cultural and social bonds between Doolin and Inisheer. Occasionally music sessions began in O'Connor's and finished up in Inisheer.

SAILING TO INISHEER, 1972
BILL O'BRIEN (WITH BEARD),
GERRY O'FLAHERTY, INISHEER (FOREGROUND)

Morning-after party with Jamsie Caoillte

As Doolin's popularity rose, the economic health of the area improved. Emigration slowed, or at least became seasonal. There was a jaunty air about the place and a lot of music. At that time, O'Connor's pub was the epicenter of the fun. Gus and Doll were noted for their hospitality and friendliness. O'Connor's was more than a pub serving drink and nourishment: it was a tourist office, bank, message center and mail drop. Above all, it was a meeting place for like minds.

Music happened spontaneously in O'Connor's. It could start up at any time and for no apparent reason. There was something about the place that demanded fun, an atmosphere of warmth and welcome.

Most nights Pakie Russell was there; sometimes Willie Beg Shannon or Paddy Killoughery arrived, fiddles ready for playing. Jamsie Caoilte was seldom absent; in long black coat, he was always game to dance. Rory O'Connor, Pakie Moloney, Michael Egan and Michael Sherlock sat at the bar. There were always stories, sometimes old, other times embellished gossip told with style and panache. On good nights, Sherlock sang 'By the Waves of the Silvery Tide.' Pakie called for his concertina, centuries melted away and magic happened.

There were great nights when well-known musicians from far-flung places came to pay their respects to the Doolin masters. Folk musicians, rock musicians and classical musicians all came. Porter flowed and connections were made. There were memorable sessions when members of The Bothy Band or De Danann dropped by for a few tunes. Matt Molloy and Tommy Peoples playing with Paddy Killoughery and Pakie. Paddy Keenan and Gusie Russell swopping jigs. Frankie Gavin, Alec Finn and Micho Russell reeling it out in a corner. In retrospect, this was the Golden Age of Doolin, the last flash of a society not quiet ready for the next century.

The ratio of locals to visitors changed by the late 1970s, as more and more came to Doolin: Europeans in yellow rain-wear and green rucksacks; lost Americans in rental cars; Irish businessmen with bimbos; politicians and lobbyists; artists and academics; drunks and punks; film stars and the love starved; preachers and leeches. Brought there by word of mouth, they came in droves during the summer and all had a good time. Doolin was exotic, chic and cosmopolitan, with endless revelry and a stream of interesting visitors. Cultural tourists on the counter-culture trail. And just like Francis MacNamara had made rules taboo in the 1910s, there was an atmosphere of laissez-faire about Doolin in these golden years.

As Irish music gained popularity in Europe, Micho Russell was frequently invited to perform there and his unique, simple style and presence further spread the mystique of Doolin.

The scene was inter-generational and young and old sported and played together: Gusie Russell and young Michael and P.J. Hynes swapped jigs and reels in a corner, while Jamsie Caoilte danced with Swedish blondes.

The scene was spread between Fisherstreet and Roadford. Hostels opened, restaurants, cafes, craftshops followed. With neither bus nor rail service to Doolin, many hitchhiked there and very few left on schedule. Doolin was heaven, Woodstock in Clare. Just as the Celtic Twilight lingered on in Doolin, so did the '60s.

On summer nights, crowds packed the pubs to capacity and locals were uncomfortable when they came for a late pint. Pakie Russell often came down to O'Connor's to see a handsome German lady, or maybe a starry-eyed young American man sitting in his *sugán* chair. It seemed his refuge was taken over by strangers. Doolin was already famous when Pakie died in 1977. He was one of the tradition-bearers who made it so, and the first of his generation to pass away. It seemed to happen with sudden starkness.

THE LARGE number of music lovers coming to the area was the catalyst for the Lisdoonvarna Folk Festival, launched in 1978 by locals Paddy Doherty and Jim Shannon. After the first year the event moved closer to Doolin and was re-branded The Lisdoonvarna Music Festival. It drew hundreds of thousands of young people every year and a sizable number never went to the festival but schmoozed and boozed in the Doolin pubs. The event always had a traditional music component and Micho Russell once played a memorable set of tunes with a Belgian 'nature dancer.'

Piper Séamus Ennis returned to Doolin to play at the festival in 1982, one of his last public perfor-

MICHAEL SHERLOCK AND THREE HAPPY LADIES, O'CONNOR'S, 1975

STEVIE MACNAMARA, PRIMAL BEATS

mances. The event came to an unfortunate end in 1983 after a bikers' brawl and unrelated tragic drownings at Ballaghaline.

DURING THE 1980S Doolin featured in 'Time' magazine, German newspapers and Japanese television. It became known as the best place in Ireland to experience authentic traditional Irish music. There was a huge demand for music in the region. The scene was infectious and fostered a new generation of young musicians who came to play and learn from the Russells and the Killougherys: Michael and P.J. Hynes, Christy Barry, Noel Hill, Tony Linnane, James Devitt, Davy Spillane, Eoin O'Neill, Eugene Lambe, Kevin Griffin, Sharon Shannon, Mary Custy, Terry Bingham and many more, served their time in Doolin. Travel guidebooks gave it 'essential visit' status and it got a bus service. Doolin had arrived.

Tourists came expecting music. Publicans couldn't depend on spontaneity to provide tunes, so they retained musicians. Crowds increased and little by little the dynamics of the pub session changed. Tunes were played for the tourists' benefit rather than solely for the community.

Writing in the early 1990s, broadcaster and musicologist P.J. Curtis noted:[25]

A visit to any of the three music pubs—O'Connor's, McGann's or McDermott's—may now often seem like stepping into some great pan-European gathering. Swedes rub shoulders with Italians, Germans with Bretons and Australians with Americans. It is not uncommon to catch sight of foreign hitchers on the roads out of Dublin carrying cards with the word 'Doolin' written on them.

LOCALS QUIETLY MENTION that the Old Doolin slipped away with the tragic death of Micho Russell in 1994. His passing coincided with the heating-up of the Irish economy, the branding of a New Ireland and Riverdance. All the old Doolin tradition-bearers had passed before the Celtic Tiger mauled the country.

Of all the traditional arts, music and dancing are the last to survive in Doolin. They have outlived *sean-nós* singing, storytelling, and even the Irish language. They are the last flowers in the garden; we hadn't the sun, but we had the tunes. When you see the crowds coming to Doolin nowadays, it's mind-boggling to consider that they're here mostly because of a handful of musicians who played

DOOLIN BANJO PLAYER, KEVIN GRIFFIN

Session in McGann's, summer, 1992

tunes in O'Connor's bar. They were the real tradition-bearers. Apart from what good fortune these men brought to Doolin, their influence on Irish traditional musicians and listeners worldwide is remarkable.

By 2016, the background scenery is still the same around Doolin, but the old thatch and flag roofed cottages are well outnumbered and dwarfed by new houses. There are now hotels in the parish, a new pub, new shops, restaurants, cafes, hostels, taxis, ferry companies, ticket offices, the whiff of tourism and a few scars from the Boom Years. Visitors come year-round and there's a thriving local community. The profile of the tourist has changed from hippies and folkies to mainstream holiday makers with credit cards. Tourists come in big buses and pubs serve more meals than pints of porter. Most nights there's music in the pubs and the odd party to keep things going after closing time.

When time caught up with Doolin, the old tradition bearers had moved on. It was a powerful blast, but everything changes. The photos on pub walls are like reminders at a holy shrine — Pakie, Gusie and Micho Russell, with their friends Paddy and John Killoughery, Willie Beg, Rory O'Connor and others.

Much of their lore and art died with these tradition-bearers. All were bachelors and had no kin to pass their gifts to, unlike the musicians of nearby Miltown Malbay or Kilfenora. Still, many of their tunes and capers were picked up by young local musicians and some from the surrounding areas. To the tuned ear, Paddy Killoughery's

SEÁN O'CONNOR
SEPTEMBER 1998, BEFORE THE PUB CHANGED OWNERSHIP

lift and Micho Russell's phrasing can be still heard in pub sessions when the chemistry is right.

Many academics have visited the area since Séamus Delargy arrived in 1928. Some have collected folklore, tunes and songs for preservation, others have studied the community and family life. In recent years a number have written about Doolin's transition from cultural oasis to tourist mecca.

American anthropologist Adam Kaul has written a Ph.D. thesis about the traditional music, tourism and social change in Doolin at the Millennium.[26]

Sociologists Kieran Keohane and Carmen Kuhling mention Doolin in their work, their kindest remark being: *The good is gone out of it*,[27]

Clare-born Gearóid Ó hAllmhuráin, an anthropologist and ethnomusicologist noted that:

> Doolin today is a paradoxical cultural sanctuary, where musical pilgrims have supplanted the musical icons they came to worship…While the fling is still in full flight in Doolin its musical Esperanto is more a requiem for a lost past than an anthem for a saved future.[28]

BUT NO MATTER what academics or critics might think or say, the beat goes on in Doolin and anyone who comes here has a memorable visit. Each February, Irish musicians gather for the Russell Weekend. A commemoration and a celebration, it's always a very special time. Maybe it's the old spirits or ghosts, ear to door waiting for a few bars of "The Boy in the Gap."

Somehow, music sounds sweeter here. The ground is alive with generations of tunes, songs, steps and tales; folk art that has seeped back into the landscape that inspired it. People, place and culture: That's the *draíocht*, the magic of Doolin.

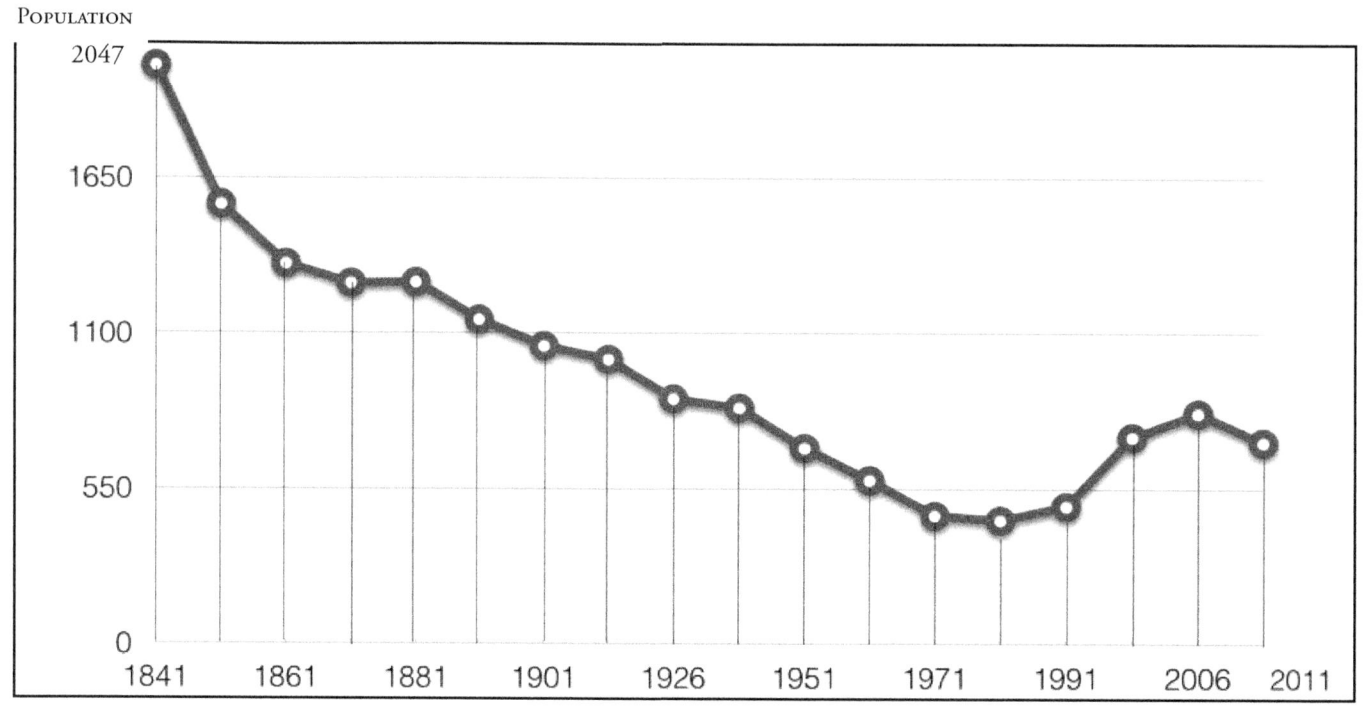

POPULATION OF DOOLIN: 1841-2011

Photo Credits

P. 8 ©Michael FitzGerald, photographer

P. 10 MacNamara Collection, Courtesy Clare County Library

P. 12 MacNamara Collection, Courtesy Clare County Library

P. 14 ©Michael FitzGerald, photographer

P. 16 ©Michael FitzGerald, photographer

P. 18 ©Michael FitzGerald, photographer

P. 20 ©Michael FitzGerald, photographer

P. 22 ©Michael FitzGerald, photographer

P. 23 Lawrence Collection, ©National Library of Ireland

P. 24 Lawrence Collection, ©National Library of Ireland

P. 25 Westropp Collection, Courtesy Clare County Library

P. 26 Lawrence Collection, ©National Library of Ireland

P. 27 Westropp Collection, Courtesy Clare County Library

P. 28 Lawrence Collection, ©National Library of Ireland

P. 31 Seán O'Connor, Fisherstreet, Doolin

P. 32 Ellen Murphy, Maine, USA

P. 34 *The Caves of North-West Clare, Ireland*: University of Bristol Speleological Society, UK

P. 35 Lawrence Collection, ©National Library of Ireland

P. 36 ©Michael John Glynne, Courtesy Clare County Library

P. 37 Seán O'Connor, Fisherstreet, Doolin

P. 38 Seán O'Connor, Fisherstreet, Doolin

P. 38 Doolin Ferry; www.doolinferry.com

P. 39 Seán O'Connor, Fisherstreet, Doolin

P. 40 ©Michael John Glynne, Courtesy Clare County Library (both photos)

P. 41 Seán O'Connor, Fisherstreet, Doolin

P. 42 ©Richard Gibson, Los Angeles, USA

P. 43 Seán O'Connor, Fisherstreet, Doolin

References

1. www.burrentolkiensociety.ie

2. John, Augustus, *Chicaroscuro*, Johnathan Cape, 1952, pp. 80

3. Frost, James, *The History and Topography of the County of Clare*,- CLASP, Clare Library online. http://tinyurl.com/ldeo35u

4. *Petty's Census of Clare, 1659*: Baroney of Corcomroe, Parish of Killiliagh. CLASP, Clare Library online. http://tinyurl.com/k5gu85q

5. *Mason's Parochial Survey, 1814-1819*. Union of Kilmanaheen, Kilasbuglenane, Kilmacreehy, Killilagh and Kilmoon. CLASP, Clare Library online. http://tinyurl.com/o4plp74

6. *Irish Education Enquiry, 1824*- Killeelagh [Killilagh] Parish. CLASP, Clare Library online. http://tinyurl.com/13m3qu5

7. *The Parliamentary Gazetteer of Ireland, 1845: Killilagh*. CLASP, Clare Library online. http://tinyurl.com/m3nycmr

8. *Poverty Before the Famine in County Clare*. CLASP, Clare Library online. http://tinyurl.com/lqx4las

9. O'Donovan, John and Curry, Eugene (1839) *Ordnance Survey Letters (Killilagh)*. CLASP, Clare Library online. http://tinyurl.com/o396k4c

10. *Leabhar Stiofáin Uí Éalaoire*; Comhairle Bhéaloideas Éireann, Dublin 1981, pp. 2-4

11. H.B.H, *Holiday Haunts on the West Coast of Clare*; 1891, McKern & Sons, Limerick. CLASP, Clare Library online. http://tinyurl.com/mt29rz3

12. *Prehistoric Remains (Fort and Dolmens) along the Borders of the Burren, in the County of Clare*: The Journal of the Royal Society of Antiquaries of Ireland, Fifth Series, Vol. 35, No.4, [Fifth Series, Vol. 15] 1905. pp. 342-361

13. *Limerick Field Club Journal*, vol ii, pp.50

14. Halpin, Sarah *The Story of Doonagore Quarry and Liscannor Stone*; The Other Clare, 32, 2009. pp. 73-78

15. John, Augustus, *Chiaroscuro—Fragments of Autobiography*; Johanathan Cape, 1952; pp. 80, County Clare

16. Delargy, Séamus, *Oral Tradition of Thomond*; Eugene O'Curry lecture, University College Dublin, November 29, 1962

17. Arensberg, Conrad M. and Kimbal, Solon T. *Family and Community in Ireland*, CLASP, Clare Library online. http://tinyurl.com/4h3qp

18. *The Journal of the Royal Society of Antiquaries of Ireland*, Seventh Series, Vol. 5, No.1, June 30, 1935), pp. 148

19. *A Bronze Zoomorphic Brooch and Other Objects from Toomullin, Co. Clare:* Joseph Raftery; The Journal of the Royal Society of Antiquaries of Ireland, seventh Series, Vol. 11, No. 2 (Jun. 30, 1941), pp. 56-60

20. *ITA Topographical and General Survey*, Corcomroe & Burren, Killilagh parish, 1937. CLASP, Clare Library online. http://tinyurl.com/or57kl

21. *Going to the Well for Water: The Séamus Ennis Field Diary 1942-1946*, Editor, Prof. Ríonach uí Ógáin, Director of the National Folklore Collection, pp. 311

22. *The Caves of North-West Clare, Ireland*: (1964) University of Bristol Speleological Society

23. Coady, Michael, *The Well of Spring Water: A memoir of Pakie and Micho Russell*, 1996. pp. 15

24. *Ireland: A Nation's Memory*, French 3rd Channel Documentary, 1973. Produced by Claude Fleouter & Roviros Manthoulis. View at http://youtu.be/sUy57dtThzM

25. Curtis, PJ *Notes from the Heart*, Torc, Dublin, 1995

26. Kaul, Adam R. *The Limits of Commodification in Traditional Irish Music Sessions;* The Journal of the Royal Anthropological Institute, Vol. 13, No. 3, 2007 pp. 703-719 (A*lso: Turning the Tune*; Adam R. Kaul, Bergahn Books, USA)

27. *Collision Culture,* Keohane, Kieran & Kuhling, Carmen; Liffey Press, Dublin, 2009

28. *Doolin Dischord: Musical Devolution in an Irish Micro Soundscape*, Gearóid hAllmhuráin; Béasana 8, UCC, 2009. pp.

29. The old Doolin music is commemorated every year at the Russell weekend in February. The gathering always has the spark of the famous sessions of the 70s and 80s. www.michorussellweekend.ie

Resources

Doolin Guide & Map by Martin Breen is an invaluable resource. It shows sites of both cultural and historical interest as well as information on tourist services in Doolin. http://tinyurl.com/kyaqhbp. Also available from Amazon

Clare County Library has several online publications which give additional information on Doolin culture and heritage. See http://tinyurl.com/p42g6z7

FISHERSTREET VILLAGE AND BRIDGE, 1950S

The Way We Were

A SLIGHT MAN with twinkling eyes, cap sideways on his head, Paddy Pharaic Mhichil Shannon was the last native Irish speaker in Doolin. He lived alone in a small thatched cottage behind O'Connor's pub, a half-mile or so from the sea. The cottage was built by his father on the site of an older cottage, which was razed by fire. All the materials used were local: stone and floor flags from the local quarries, wood from Ennistymon and Killshanny reeds for thatch. It's the youngest thatch cottage in the village, he used say.

Paddy's kitchen had a flagstone floor and was sparsely furnished: an old brown dresser displayed a few Willow Pattern plates and jugs, and by the window, there was a small table covered with a yellow oilcloth and a couple of wooden chairs. The white-washed walls were bare apart from a Carmelite Sisters' calendar and a picture of the Last Supper above the hearth. Over the door, small rush crosses, brown from smoke and age, lined the edges of the ceiling. Heat came from a huge open fireplace—about six feet wide, with hobs on either side. A small scruffy cat slept on one, an old black kettle on the other hob. In the grate a mound of turf glowed orange-red. This was the only light in the kitchen. Paddy declined electricity, and his most modern appliances were a small transistor radio and a small tabletop two-burner gas stove.

PADDY PHARAIC MHICHIL SHANNON
(1916 - 1992)

The following is from conversations that we had over the years. Sometimes they were in Irish, other times a mixture of both languages. Irish sections here have been translated into English as Paddy spoke it for the purpose of the narrative.

When you think of it, sure, English is new around these parts. 'Twas all Irish they spoke in this village and around when I was young. My father and mother hadn't much English until we went to school; they learned most of what they knew from us, sure. The Irish was spoken here in Fisherstreet by the people the longest...of course it was the language of the sea and the fishin', and goin' in and out to Aran. We had more use for it than the people in the country. That time, in the summer evenings, the women and children would gather at the river wall in Fisherstreet, and all the talk would be in Irish. After a while someone might sing a song in Irish and that's how the time was passed while we waited for the fishermen to come home from the shore.

'Twas a pity the Irish died out, an awful lot was lost, all the old songs and recitations and of course the stories, these will never be heard again. And all the *sean-fhocals* (proverbs) and cures and prayers and things, these are all lost now and more's the pity, because they were very useful. Names are gone for things and there's things now and there's no names for them in English.

But of course Irish wasn't seen as much use if you had to leave here. Sure, back then, when I was young, there was someone goin' to America every second day, times were hard. That was the saddest thing about them days—all the people who had to leave the place, God help us. Most of them never returned. They had big goin' away nights but they were sad too.

There was no music in the pubs when I was young, 'twas all in the cottages. People hadn't much money to spend on drink in those days. Most of the pubs around here would hardly sell six barrels of porter in a year. Now sure, they'd sell that much in a night. When we were young, a lot of people drank *poitín* around here. I don't know how much of it was made locally but I know men in this village used to get it from Connemara. The Connemara men would bring it as far as Inisheer and the Fisherstreet crowd would pick it up there. The *poitín* was great, especially for cures. Good *poitín* would cure anything and it was great for sick animals.

Even though times were hard when we were young, they were the best of times and it's now we can see they were the best. People were much happier even though they were poor, but neighbours were good. I remember seein' women from the country coming down here to Fisherstreet with buckets of buttermilk on their heads and butter swimmin' in the milk. We had no cows here in the village at the time and butter was a Godsend. These women went from house to house dolin' out butter and went back home with as much fish as they could carry.

We depended a lot on the sea. All the fishermen lived in this village, that's how it got the name Fisherstreet. The old people said that long 'go there was houses on the other side of the road, right on the riverbank. When we were young the fishing was great, a lot of the catch used to be exported to England—flatfish, mackerel, cod, pollock and ling. We fished a lot with hand lines and spillers. 'Tis only lately that the lobster fishing started. Sure, years ago Cuckoo

Death of a Language

In 1926, Irish was the everyday language of many older adults around Doolin and the area was deemed a *Gaeltacht*, or Irish-speaking district by the government. English was the language of commerce and many parents considered it the first step to a better way of life for their children. Scars of the Great Famine, centuries of colonialism, the realities of emigration, and social and economic circumstances of the time, made English seem more progressive, practical and desirable. Parents encouraged their children to learn and use English rather than their native language. In Clare, bit by bit, the transmission link was weakening and little of the old language flowed to the young generation. The best that could be hoped for was to preserve a record of how it was spoken and the culture it carried with it.

In 1929 when Séamus Delargy of *Cumann Béaloideas Éireann* (the Folklore of Ireland Society), came to Doolin to collect stories of the area, a good number of native speakers were still alive. Delargy was highly impressed by the quality of their Irish which he thought was the purest he had ever heard. He later wrote:

> "It was Irish which for richness of vocabulary and wealth of idiom had few rivals. The dead words on a manuscript page are a poor substitute for the haunting beauty of the language which lingered and died on the lips of my old friends."[1]

Delargy considered storyteller Stiofán Uí Ealaoire the finest Irish speaker he had ever come across and in 1936, he arranged for Stiofán and other Doolin native speakers to travel to University College Galway and have their Irish recorded on shellac discs.[2]

In the same year, writing about the townland of Luogh in Doolin, Conrad Arensberg tells us: "Its language, at least of the old people, is Irish, but the young are forgetting the old tongue. English is the more common speech today, even here."[3]

DOOLIN IRISH SPEAKER Seán MacMathúna was an assistant to Father Clune, when he was studying Clare Irish in 1940 for his book *Caint an Chláir* (Language of Clare). Fr. Clune described a dire situation where only the elderly in remote areas spoke Irish.[4]

When Nils M. Holmer surveyed the Irish dialects of Clare in 1946, he had 22 informants in Luogh and 14 in Fisherstreet.[4] As the older generation passed away, the number of Irish speakers got fewer and more dispersed. Only in Fisherstreet, where they lived closer to each other, did speakers make up any sort of community

The passing of the old language was accompanied by a decline in the oral traditions associated with it. Nights of storytelling got fewer and in a matter of decades, centuries of myth and wisdom disappeared into silence. A survey carried out by Heinrich Wagner in 1951-52 noted:

> "In Doolin and Fisherstreet, Irish is on the verge of dying although most of the older generation can speak it… English has become the vernacular of the younger generation everywhere."[5]

By the 1950s the Gaeltacht boundaries were redefined to reflect the true use of Irish in regions. The old Clare Gaeltacht was given *Breac-Gaeltacht* or bi-lingual status. Fisherstreet was the last community of Irish language speakers in County Clare.

Today there are no native Irish speakers in Doolin, though many can speak it and the language is cherished. In English speech, Irish words and idioms still colour conversation. When Aran islanders come ashore, Irish is heard in the local pubs and shops. On the top of Doonagore, a red light blinks at night on the *Radio na Gaeltachta* relay mast, signalling there's still an ember in the fire.

O'Brien was the only one who had lobster pots and he had only two or three. Nobody could afford lobsters back then, sure, apart from the priests and bishops who came on holidays to Lisdoonvarna.

THAT TIME TOO, the world of beggar men came around here, because people were good to them. All sorts of unfortunates were going the road, many of them traveling teachers, tradesmen or musicians. They had no homes and would spend a couple of nights here and then move on to some other house. They came from all over, Galway and Kerry and every place. And they came in batches, every couple of months a different one would call every day. There was a Tom Woods, a traveling scholar, a small, low little man with a big white beard and a long black coat. Murphy the Fiddler used to come around and sometimes another man called The Murtach came with him. The Murtach was as strong as a horse and taught dancing. He was a bit fond of the drink and could only last a few days anywhere before people got tired of him.

A traveling teacher came around here one time and a local girl ran away with him, she was a strong pupil. Anyway, a few years later, didn't they come back and settle beyond in Luogh where he set up a school for his own children. So, the officials didn't like this, the English were in charge here at the time and they sent an officer up to the schoolteacher. The man they sent up had a bad leg, he was shot in some foreign war and that is how he got the job, but he wasn't very smart.

"Why aren't you sending your children to school?" He asked.

"If you answer this question," the schoolteacher said, "I'll send them to where ever you say."

He handed the officer the question written out on a slate. The officer couldn't make head nor tail out of it and then the teacher gave it to one of the children and he worked it out in a flash.

TOURING CYCLISTS AT ROADFORD BRIDGE, LATE 1940S

"Now," said the schoolteacher, "when you learn how many fours are in sixty-four, come back and we'll talk again.

The longest memories I have are of Christmas. We'd be getting ready for Christmas for weeks. There used to be great excitement. The house would be cleaned from top to bottom and decorated with holly and ivy. There used to be big markets in Ennistymon and my mother would go there with other women from the village. That would be their biggest shopping day of the year. We'd be down at the bridge, waitin' for them to come home and wonderin' what they'd bring us back. If we got jam and baker's bread we'd be over the moon. We never got toys or do-das, but all the same we had plenty to play with. I remember gettin' a small piece of currant cake from my mother one Christmas Eve and goin' down to the street so the other children would see it, I was that proud of it. Even though money was scarce, Christmas was much nicer then, a lot of the old customs are gone and forgotten now.

Except for the gentry, Christmas was the only time in the year that people here got a letter or a card. A lot of money came from America and other places then. Sometimes parcels arrived too, mostly with clothes. On Christmas Eve, before we had the tea, my father would gather us in the kitchen to light the Christmas candle. It was the youngest of the family that always lit it and I remember my father holdin' my hand to do it. He used to say a prayer in Irish, to welcome Mary and Joseph to the house if they happened to be passin'. From that candle, other ones were

---

Dec 23/1896

Mr Ned Lafferty by <u>Cash</u>

3lb tea	7/4
2st sugar	4/-
2lb raisins	10
2lb currants	8
3 large red candles	9
1/2 doz candles	3
1/4 oz white pepper	3
1/2 oz carraways	3
starch	1

Patrick Kelly

1 sack Flour	1/12/-
1 quart Malt	5/-

Mrs Moughan

1 st sugar	2/-
1 st flour	1/8
1 quart rum	5/-
1 quart malt	5/-
2 gals stout	3/4
3 red candles	9

Mr Tobin

1/2 Pint Malt	1/2
4 drinks	91/2
1/2 pint malt	1/2

Extract from Considine's shop ledger, Christmas, 1896

lit and put in the windows. Every family did the same, and it was beautiful to look across the countryside and see all the little lights in the cottages. I remember walkin' to Mass on Christmas morning with my mother and father when I was very young. It was pitch dark and there was a candle lighting in the window of every cottage. All the people goin' to Mass were talkin' Irish and givin' blessings to each other. I'll never forget that.

IT WOULD STILL BE dark on St. Stephen's morn when you'd hear horns blowin', callin' the Wren Boys. If you looked out the window, you'd see all the candles bein' lit in the cottages all around. The Wren Boys used gather below at the bridge in Fisherstreet, they might be thirty or forty people in the batch, between dancers and players and an *amadán* (male fool/clown) and an *oinseach* (female fool). They'd be dressed up with coats turned inside out and crossed with ribbons of green and gold. Stepheneen Hardy was their leader when I was young and he rode a black ass.

The Wren Boys would travel the country that day and come back here at night. We'd hear the noise of them comin' and everyone would go down to the bridge to meet them. Stepheneen would lead them through Fisherstreet and stop below outside O'Connor's pub. That was their last stop. There used to be great excitement and of course 'twould go on for hours, music, set dancin' and a bit of singin'.

AMADÁN AND OINSEACH

MY FATHER played the flute and he had a lot of old tunes. He bought me a concertina in Ennistymon and I learned it for a while and then stopped. And I don't know why I stopped. My sister took it up then and when she left for Australia she brought the concertina with her. 'Tis now I'm sorry I didn't stick at it, if only to keep my father's tunes alive. They're lost forever now.

In those days there was a concertina in every second house and they used to keep them in a little nook by the open fire to keep the reeds and the bellows dry. Most women could play a few tunes on the concertina but seldom played outside the house; 'twas they taught the youngsters to play. We were spoiled with the best of music around here—Stepheneen Hardy, Pádraig Flanagan, the Russells, the Killougherys, Willie Beg and Michileen. And God only knows how many others left for America and brought the music with them.

The best of the musicians were never recorded and it's a pity because they were right geniuses. Pádraig Flanagan could make the concertina sing. They called him 'Sober' because he seldom drank and used to sit straight like a teacher. The only part of him that moved were his hands and you'd never know to look at his face that he was playing such beautiful music. And he never broke a concertina, he never tore a bellows.

Paddy Pharaic Mhichil keeping the home fire burning, 1981

STEPHENEEN HARDY was another genius. Himself and Flanagan used play together and 'tis they who first made Doolin famous for dancin' and music. Stepheneen was pure gifted and played the fiddle and the concertina. They say he got his music from 'The Otherside', like a great lot of the older musicians around here long 'go. In return for the Gift, Stepheneen was *'overlooked'* by *them*, the fairies, *na Daoine Maithe*, or 'the good people', spirits I s'pose you'd call them. They gave Stepheneen the Gift, but he was crossed with a cork leg from the knee down. A fine looking fella, but fierce wicked when he had drink taken. During the month of September he used to ride a black ass bareback into Lisdoonvarna and play for visitors at the Spa Wells, collecting whatever few pence he could. He made enough to buy a small cart for the ass.

But anyways, when bicycles became all the rage he had to buy one. He even got a special pedal fitted for the bad leg. But the poor man couldn't manage the bicycle when he had drink taken; he used to be falling off it and hurting himself. For a finish, he damaged himself so bad that he ended up in Ennistymon Hospital. He was there for a good while and put up a great battle. And then one night he asked for his fiddle and played an almighty blast of music that cured all that was in the ward. He was dead himself the next morning, the poor man. And he only thirty-four or five years of age.

A LOT OF THESE gifted musicians are *overlooked*, so they're highly strung and naturally wicked. I don't know in the world why, but maybe the music is the cause of it. Some of them do be at all kinds of capers when they are playing, but they can't help it, the *craturs*. It's the music breaking out through them.

But of course, people used to say that fairies are very fond of music and I'm thinkin' that's why there was so many of *them* here around Doolin. I often heard it said that there was more of *them* around here than anywhere else in Munster. My father said *they* are people from this world who're still stuck here, even though they're dead. More people say they are descendants of the De Danann who lived around here long, long ago. People only stopped believing in fairies recently, but they're still around, even if they're getting scarce. Of course, they can help you too, if you had the courage to talk to them and do what they ask. But that isn't easy because the words stick in your throat when you meet them.

LONG AGO there used to be cottages right down on the banks of the river in Fisherstreet. A lot of the fishermen and their families lived there, God help us, and they were supposed to be very poor houses. One day in the spring a few of the men who lived down there went into Aran with bonhams and they stayed late, drinkin' I s'pose. But on the way back anyway a storm rose and they were lost, never to be seen again. 'Twas a great tragedy, a big loss to this part of the country.

A while afterwards, didn't one of the wives wake up of a night. She heard footsteps in the room, she heard the squelching of wet shoes and then she saw her drowned husband and he drippin' with water. He told her not to come near him, but there was a way she could bring him back—on a certain night, at a certain time, he'd be passing by with a crowd of fairies and all she had to do was throw a fistful of clay at him and she'd break the spell and bring him back. He warned her not to tell anybody about this; if she did, he said the game was up. She promised not to say a word about it, but of course, with all the excitement, she had to tell the other wives.

On the night, she was at the right place with her fistful of clay and she hid behind a bush until she heard them coming on horses. Just as they were passing she threw the clay at her husband and he just turned and looked at her and shouted,

"You should have listened to me. It's too late. Goodbye now, I'm gone forever."

I STILL BELIEVE IN FAIRIES. You'd have to, sure, after seeing and hearing about the strange things that happened around here. When we were young, a crowd of us put our money together and bought a leather football from a hawker who came to Ennistymon on fair days. 'Twas lovely, a great rarity, because all we had for kickin' was a sock filled with hay or a pig's bladder. Anyway, one evening there was a game of football below in a field between the road and the river—*Pairc ó Thuaidh* it's called. There was a crowd of us in it and someone kicked the ball up in the sky and when it hit the ground, it never bounced but disappeared. Gone. Just like you'd blow out a candle. Well of course we searched and searched and just when 'twas nearly getting dark, a strange priest on a bicycle came over the road and called us. I can still see him in my mind's eye, a lovely little man, grey hair, a bit bald on the forehead, and a big mud lasher on the front of the bike.

"What are ye looking for?" He asked.

We told him and he said,

"Ye'll never find that ball and come outa that field quick or the rest of ye might disappear. Ye couldn't be in a worse place, that field is haunted."

He started to get a bit cross so we hurried off home and he went away on his bicycle, down towards the shore. Of course the word spread like wildfire and all the villagers waited for him to come back over the road. But he never did. Himself and the bicycle disappeared. I gave a description of him to everyone and they said it sounded like Father O'Keeffe from Kilkenny, who was drowned below at the shore a few years before.

But the strange thing was, the next morning when the fishermen were getting up to go fishing, 'twas still dark, they heard shouting and cheering outside and couldn't know what it was. They knew it was coming from *Pairc ó Thuaidh* and they stood below at the butt of the lane-way listening, until dawn broke. And then they saw what was happening, a big football match watched by a huge crowd. They recognised some of them, people who had died over the years. 'Tis them who took the football.

IT'S SAFER to be good to the fairies. People often left potatoes outside in case they were hungry. This was done especially if there was a death in the house. And fairies were always under the bed a corpse was laid out on, listening to prayers. Some old women used put the basin of water the corpse was washed in under the bed to distract them from stealing prayers for the dead. You'll always find them around a corpse house.

May Eve was a time when fairies were everywhere. There was a woman dying beyond in Luogh one May Eve and when the priest arrived, he was in a terrible state. He said they were all over the place, sitting on the walls by the side of the road, more hoppin' and jumpin' in the haggard. The priest himself was afraid to leave the house and spent the night there saying rosaries and other prayers. Fairies are always out and about on May Eve, and I s'pose when they knew someone was dying they all came to the house to see the soul departing.

The same thing happened in this village. A young girl got very sick on May Eve and they put her to bed by the fire. The father went out to get help from an old healer woman who lived beyond in Roadford and was great with children.

On the way back home, they saw the *sí gaoithe* (the fairy wind), and the old woman knew they had the child taken. She said nothing to the father, she was afraid that he might try and follow them because that would be the worst thing you could do.

Anyway when they came to the house, the old woman lifted up the blankets and peeped in under them. All that was left was a tiny sick child, thin as a stick. The fairies took the real child and left a changeling in her place. They did that.

And of course they're always out at Samhain or Halloween. It's only a night to stay at home by the fire. Often *they* try to go back to the homes where they had lived, the poor souls. Samhain is a dangerous night to be out, because you might meet a dead relation who'd recognise you and God only knows what might happen to you. A terrible night for getting lost, and a terrible night for going astray.

THERE WAS A WOMAN living here long 'go and Boetius MacClancy appeared to her one night when she was in bed. She recognised who 'twas because he had one leg narrower than the other. He frightened the life outa her so the next day she went to the priest and told him what happened. The priest gave her a bottle of holy water and said to sprinkle it around the bed and that would protect her and keep him away from her. So anyway she did that, and didn't Boetius appear the next night again. She asked him what he wanted but he didn't answer. Then she said, in Irish,

"What narrowed your leg, Boetius MacClancy?"

"Being unkind to the poor and evicting a widow with

three sheep, that's what narrowed my leg," he said.

"And where's your treasure, Boetius MacClancy?" she asked him.

"It's seven leaps of a warrior from the river to the stone, that's where my treasure is buried."

That's what he said, seven leaps of a warrior from the river to the stone covering the treasure. So there was the clue. Of course after that lots of people went searching for the treasure, but it was never found. People got other clues as well, mainly from dreams.

But of course the trouble about finding anything like treasure is that the fairies guard it. There's always someone mindin' money, whether they're dead or alive. So if you're goin' searchin', there's certain things you'd want to bring with you: a black-handled knife is very lucky, a sheaf of hay or straw, Holy Water or water from a forge.

And there's other things too you have to watch out for as well. I remember a woman who lived near us here a good few years ago, having a dream about where Boetius buried the gold. Three or four nights in a row she dreamed of it and knew the exact place and all, between the river and the castle. So, you see, it's not the dreamer who finds the treasure at all but the first person that they tell. The dreamer should never go looking for buried treasure, oh my God, but that's a terrible dangerous thing to do.

But anyway, she told Tom Mac, so himself and a few more went over and brought all the things with them. They

started digging and when they came across an old stone candle-holder, they knew then they were in luck, because that was in her dream. So they took it up and sprinkled the holy water on the ground underneath and started to dig again. About four or five feet down, they hit a huge flag and knew they were close. But as soon as they touched it, they heard a loud racket out in the field and one of them jumped up out of the hole and there coming across the field was an army on horses, coming at high speed with spears and everything. Maybe they were the Spanish from the Armada that Boetius hung, I'm not sure. Well, Tom and the lads ran for all they were worth and brought the candle-holder with them, it's in some house in this village yet. I saw it myself.

I WENT HUNTIN' for Boetius' treasure myself when I was young. A woman who was married to a relation of mine had the same dream three nights in a row that gold was buried beyond in the corner of the *Teampall Beag* (Small Church), near the river. The old church is there yet, in ruins of course. When we heard about it—and we knew the exact place—a few of us decided to go lookin'. So, one Sunday at the hour of Mass, we went searchin'. During Mass is a good time because fairies often leave the treasure and hide around churches in the hope of catching a few prayers that might bring them to heaven.

We had all the things with us, the straw, black-handled

knife and the holy water. So I made a ring first with the water and said a prayer and the diggin' started. Well, we were only down two or three feet when we came across a skeleton, bones as white as snow and a skull full of teeth. So what ever got into him, didn't one of the lads take four of the teeth and put them into his pocket, to bring him luck.

Treasure Country:
Aille river cascades at Toomullin

But as soon as he did, we heard the most lonesome crying coming up from the ground. Oh my God but it was terrible and it coming right up from the earth. We just jumped up out of the hole and scooted home, left shovels and straw and knife and the lot behind. We never went back for the gold. But the strange thing was, that lad who took the four teeth grew up to be a great card player and won all around him for miles. Maybe that was the treasure we were supposed to find, you'd never know.

Sometimes fairies travel in the *sí gaoithe,* a sort of whirlwind that raises dust from the ground as it passes—anything in its way will be thrown to the sky. I've often seen it and if you had the courage to go near it, you'd hear *them* talking and know where they were going. Like the banshee, the *sí gaoithe* is around sometimes when there's a death due. The best thing to do if you see the *sí gaoithe,* is to lie down in the shelter of a wall, stay away from it.

Of course *they* can be anywhere, that's their power. My own cousin Tomaseen Mac was out fishing one night with three others and to bait their hooks, they went ashore to *Trá Lathan,* a lovely strand under the cliffs. It was a fine moonlit night and they only started cutting bait, when one of them saw a big three-masted sailing ship just beyond the waves. It appeared from nowhere, all lit up with lanterns, and they all saw it sailing between the rocks where no boat could swim. If only one fisherman saw it, you could say it was the imagination, but they all saw it and heard voices. Well, Tomaseen said they watched that ship for an hour, frightened out of their lives that it might take them away. Then it faded away and vanished. When they arrived home the next morning with the story, the old people said it was a ghost ship from *Killstuipheen,* the sunken city out from Hag's Head.

When we were young 'twas our greatest fear that we might see *Killstuipheen* when we'd be goin' or comin' from the Aran Islands. 'Twas supposed to appear every seven years, and if you saw it you died within twelve months. I remember a man called Nestor saw *Killstuipheen* one morning when he was herding cattle down near Liscannor. The poor man got a terrible stammer and he died after a few weeks. The old people said that you'd hear the church bells ringing first, and you should turn away before the spire appeared, so as not to see it. *Killstuipheen* is supposed to be a beautiful place and I heard it was covered by a big glass roof and was full of gold and silver and God only knows what else. Maybe it's like *Tír na n-Óg* as well, because some people could go there without dying. But only special people—the child of a couple with webbed feet or fingers. 'Twas said that that child would find the key to the door of a cave that went from somewhere around Moher to *Killstuipheen*. This key was supposed to be at the bottom of a lake that's on the top of Mount Callan, *Loch na Gréine* I'm thinkin' 'tis called.

ONE TIME, a couple with webbed feet got married and lived beyond in Luogh. He was from there and I'm thinkin' she was from the Kilfenora side. Anyway they had a son and of course everyone expected he'd go and look for the key when he was big. But he didn't, and I don't know why because he could have been a lucky child. He joined the priesthood instead. But two days or so before the poor boy was to be ordained, he dropped dead suddenly. The family was in a terrible way. So anyway, he was brought home and buried and his books came with him. Sometime after that the mother had a dream and he appeared and told her to bring his books to a certain field near here on a certain day. She did, and as soon as they were spread on the grass, the *sí gaoithe* came and lifted a certain book from the rest and took it off to heaven. He probably wanted that book, you'd never know. If he'd gone looking for the key to *Killstuipheen* things might have turned out a bit different for him, but maybe the poor lad was afraid he might find it.

WHEN I LEFT SCHOOL, I served my time with Dinny Sheehan, a carpenter who lived below beside the bridge. We made bits and pieces for everyone around here—chairs, dressers, windows, curraghs for the fishermen. There was always people coming and going from the workshop, often they just came in for a chat to pass the time. In those days nobody had a watch, there was no hurry—except you had to get a bus or a train from Ennistymon, no one bothered with the time. The old people wouldn't know what date or year it was, and most of them couldn't care less. My father was like that and he lived a lot happier. He knew the seasons and the pattern days and the holidays but he didn't believe in years and dates.

The only date I know is 1864. I have a penny with that date on it and I kept it because that's the year that a ship called *The Magpie* went up on the rocks beyond in Ballaghaline. 'Twas a battleship and was wrecked on the finest night that ever came.

The rock is called *The Magpie* ever since. What happened to that battleship was the strangest thing ever. 'Twas in the month of April, there was no breeze, not a puff and the night was so fine that a fog fell on the water around her. She just got lost and drifted onto the rocks. Then the captain got excited and started firing cannon balls at the shore, heavy balls of iron, some of them are around the village yet, in back yards thrown, like several other things from that ship. When the firing stopped the fishermen went over to the shore and there she was, thrown up on her side, a complete wreck.

THE SAILORS WERE TRYING to take everything valuable from the ship and there was a certain thing on her, some kind of winch that they couldn't move because it was too awkward and heavy. The captain offered a sack of flour to anyone who'd bring up the winch and everyone failed to stir it.

So a woman was living in Fisherstreet at the time, an awful strong woman called Bríd Shea, who had arms as big as a horse's thighs. She had a son who used to wear earrings and I think he died in Australia. Bríd said she'd carry the winch if they lifted it on her shoulders. It took four sailors to heave it on her back and she carried it up to the shore, collected her bag of flour and went home. All the crew from the ship were staying down at Gore's house in Ballaghaline. The Gores were landlords and very bad landlords.

Well, on his way to the house didn't one of the officers lose a purse of gold sovereigns. A young local boy spotted it on Gore's lawn and he buried it into the ground with his heel. When things got quiet he came back and collected it. The purse had twenty gold sovereigns in it—a big fortune at the time, a sweepstake—picture getting a glass of good whiskey for three half-pennies. This young lad's family got very rich very quick and never looked back since. That shipwreck was a God-send to this village. Maybe there's luck in magpies after all.

WE WENT TO ARAN a lot when we were young, to the near island especially. It was easier to get to Aran than it was to get to Ennistymon or Lahinch and there was always somewhere in there we could stay the night. The Aran people had a great welcome for us and we knew them all because they came here with their fish and to do their shopping. And of course there were family connections, because a good few Aran people had married in here over the years.

I remember being down at the pier one Sunday, a beautiful sunny day and I was as proud as punch because I was wearing my first long pants—white cotton pants that a relation of my mother's had sent home from America. I thought I was the bee's knees in style and I decided to go into Aran with two neighbours who were taking in a local big shot. As soon as we landed inside I went my own way and visited Andy and Nonee Connelly. The men went about their business and I thought no more of them until we met on the shore to go home that evening.

If I had known they all had drink taken, I wouldn't have gotten into the curragh with them. To make matters worse, the big shot had two huge big jars of *poitín* with him and there must have been a gallon in each. The drink sent us completely off course; my neighbours could hardly lift an oar never mind row. The big shot was singing and roaring' and I must have said a hundred rosaries. I was terrified and sat on the floor of the curragh up front. I thought I'd never see my father and mother again.

The next thing I heard was waves breaking and when I looked up I got the fright of my life because we had gone in under the Cliffs of Moher. We were miles off course. It was the nearest I ever came to death. I prayed for all I was worth as we tried to get out from under these cliffs. The curragh was going round in circles on the tops of the waves and it looked like the Cliffs were going to fall down on us. We got out beyond the waves eventually. But even now when I think of it, I get the shivers.

Anyway, we survived. It was daybreak when we landed at the pier. Not one word was spoken and I ran home to be in bed before my mother or father got up. I was only going in the door when I met my father and he going fishing. He looked at me, dripping wet and my new white pants all black with tar from the curragh. He said to me,

"Aha my boy, you'll have sense from now on."

SOMETIMES THE FISHERMEN from here would go across Galway Bay as far as Connemara but that stopped after the Doolin crowd had a big row over there. Martin Caoilte and a few more from this village went over with a load of bonhams and it seems some racket broke out between themselves and the Connemaras. I suppose there was *poitín* involved. But anyways Martin Caoilte bested all who were in it; he was a tough and a powerful man. His arm was broken in the fight and yet he rowed home.

"Ballaghaline or the bottom!" he used to shout.

Well, whoever fixed that arm made a bad job of it, and after six months, Martin had to go to Sexton the bone-setter in Miltown Malbay to have it corrected. Sexton had to put a big ball under the arm and broke it twice before he could set it right. He told me afterwards that Martin was the toughest man ever to walk through his door.

"That man didn't know what pain was," Sexton said, "I broke his arm twice and he stood there and never said one word."

There'll never be people like that again. These kinds of people are all gone and an awful lot of the music and stories and the likes are gone with them. They were tough people but they had to be, because the times were tough.

References

1. Delargy, Seamus, *Notes on the Oral Tradition of Thomond*, Eugene O'Curry lecture, UCD November 29, 1962.

2. *Doegan Project*, audio of stories by Stiofáin Uí Ealaoire and other local storytellers at http://tinyurl.com/lana5bu

3. Arensberg, Conrad, *The Irish Countryman, pp. 36*

4 Clune, Fr. George, *Caint an Chláir,* (Dublin) 1940

5. *The Dialects of Co Clare*, Royal Irish Academy, Todd Lecture Series, 1962

6. Wagner, Heinrich, *Linguistic Atlas and Survey of Irish Dialects*. Dublin Institute of Advanced Studies, 1958

Photo Credits:

P. 49 Eugene Lambe

P. 52 unknown

P. 64 Canavan family, St Catherines, Doolin

P. 55 and P. 65 © National Folklore Collection, UCD

Make a hay reek at St. Catherines, 1960s

Thatching Peaitsín Mhurty Flanagan's cottage, circa 1935

The Music Makers

Although the music collector George Petrie visited Clare in 1821, there is no evidence that he came to Doolin. He was fascinated by the music of Clare and thought it had distinctive qualities not found in other counties. Some of the tunes and songs that he collected in Clare were still being aired by Micho Russell and other Doolin tradition-bearers up to the end of the 20th century. The first collector of Doolin music was Séamus Ennis, who visited there in 1945.

The old Doolin storytellers mention local pipers in their tales, but by the 1900s there were only one or two pipers in the region. According to local tradition-bearers the popular instruments of that time were concertinas, flutes and whistles, mouth organs and Jew's harps. There were a few fiddlers but no bodhrans, and plenty of singers and lilters. The music was played to be danced to, rather than to be passively listened to.

The concertina is synonymous with Clare and a favorite lady's instrument. Several Doolin women played the concertina, including Annie Russell and Nora Shannon, but never brought the instrument outside the house. During the 1920s, the greatest exponents of the instrument in the area were Pádraig 'Sober' Flanagan, Paddy 'Tarbert' Killoughery, his brother Martin, Tom Moloney, Paddy Moloney and Aughty Linnane. The Killougherys were accomplished lilters as was Annie Russell.

Stepheneen Hardy was the main fiddler and also a concertina player and a piper. A gifted musician, he had a propensity for drink and going astray. Bazer Conlon from Polnagun was also a fiddler and renowned for mimicking singers he heard on gramophone records. John McCormack was a favorite of his.

The Captain Moloney was the most renowned flute-player around Doolin and patriarch of a musical family. Other noted flute and whistle players included Patrick Fitzpatrick, Paraic Mhichil Shannon, Jimmy Moloney and Thomas Flanagan.

Singers were an important part of the music matrix and almost everyone had a song or two to air. Many of the songs were in Irish and the most influential singers were the Davoran brothers, John Devitt, John MacKeen, Dean Hynes, Michael 'Styke' O'Donoghue, Peitsín Mhurty Flanagan, Jerome and Thomas Connole, Aughty Russell and schoolteacher Tim Sexton. Aughty Russell was also a lilter and occasionally played the whistle.

Wherever there was music, there was dancing. To sport and play, it was essential to have a few steps and good dancers were revered. This is the milieu that the Russell brothers, the Killougherys, Willie Beg Shannon and Michileen Conlon and other young tradition-bearers grew up in. As the Irish language died around Doolin, these young music makers preserved the tunes, songs and ways of older generations.

They became the last tradition-bearers.

Doolin Long Ago
(The joy of music and the sadness of emigration)

The music men of Doolin
Beside the rugged shore,
Willie Beg Shannon and Sober Flanagan
Stephen Hardy from Doonagore,
Their two fiddles and concertina
Are now silent for evermore.

The Russell's and Paddy Killoughery
His brothers Thady and John,
Flute, fiddle and piccolo
The music all night went on.

On a wren dance night as the stars shone bright
High above the Atlantic roar,
We got up to our tricks at Packie Dick's
As we danced around the flagstone floor.

There was music there in the salty air
And many a sweet heart won,
To sweet strains on the button accordion
By Michilin Conlon from Poulnagun.

We then made our way at the break of day
To our homes down by the shore,
The darkest night in winter
Our young hearts wild with fear,
The roadway was always brightened
By the lighthouse on Inis Oirr.

There were sad times too as most parents knew
Way down by Queenstown quay,
When loving hearts were saying goodbye
Their tear filled eyes so sad to see,
As they stepped on board a yankee steamer
Westward bound for the Statue of Liberty.

by Paddy Fitzgerald (late of Fisherstreet)

Micho, Pakie and Gussie Russell, 1974

The Russell Brothers

Austin Rúa Russell was born in 1838 and at age thirty, he married Kate Flanagan of a well-known Doolin musical family. They had a small farm in Doonagore and a cottage that looked out over the Atlantic towards the Aran Islands. The couple had five sons: John (b.1870), Michael (b.1871), Murt (b.1880), Thomas (b.1884) and Austin (b.1892). In those years the region was mostly Irish speaking and the period was called *an droch saol* or 'the bad life' in Doolin: the living was hard after the Great Famine. John Russell emigrated to America, Michael became a teacher, Murt worked as a carpenter around North Clare, Thomas joined the British Army and was killed during the Great War. Young Aughty (Austin) inherited the home place and married Annie Moloney, a neighbor from another Doolin musical family.

Aughty and Annie also had five children: Micho (b.1915) Bridget (b. 1916) Gussie (b. 1917) Pakie (b.1920) and Mary Kate (b.1921). Both parents were Irish speakers and musical: Austin was a *sean nós* singer and a lilter, Annie sang and played the concertina. The young Russells were musical royalty—they had the 'gift' from both parents.

Irish independence didn't ease the burden of small farmers very much and Aughty worked hard on the land to provide for his family. He owned a horse and cart, a big asset at the time, and hired out to neighbours, bringing turf home from the bog, stone from the quarries and barrels of salted fish to the railway station in Ennistymon. The family occasionally worked a small quarry in Luogh that provided fine flagstone for roofs and floors.

When Micho finished school at fourteen he joined his father on the land. He also helped with hauling jobs and worked for neighbours raising walls and doing bits of thatching. Séamus Delargy recorded Aughty singing in 1929, three years before he died. Micho became responsible for the family welfare then. By that time he was also on his way to becoming a musician.

Finished with school, Gussie went to work in the quarry, taking out flags and dressing them. He learned the trade of stonemason and Pakie joined him when he left school at fourteen. It was a hard graft and poorly paid work, but they had a good feel for stonework and stuck with the trade.

All around them, the Russells saw their friends and relatives leave for England and America, and their only solace was the big going-away parties where there was music, dancing and some drink. And even though staying at home meant poverty and lack of opportunity, their rich cultural background fastened their ties to Doolin. In the local music, songs, dance, stories, customs and folklore, they found their sustenance.

All three brothers were whistle players, Micho and Gussie also played the flute and Pakie is best known as a concertina player. Their playing was spirited and rootsy, a simple style without decoration or ornamentation. Each of them sang and Pakie and Micho had songs in Irish as well as English. They were the sound of Doolin and they had the *draíocht*, that intangible musical magic to transport listeners to an older world.

Over the decades, much music was collected from the Russells, notably by Breandán Breathnach and Séamus Ennis. Ennis recorded them for Radio Éireann in the late 1940s and Ciarán MacMathúna also featured them on his traditional music programmes in the 1950s. Bit by bit the Russells' music was heard by the rest of the country.

When people began coming to Doolin in the later years, there was hardly a night when one of the brothers wasn't playing in O'Connor's in Fisherstreet. The only commercial recording of Micho, Gussie and Pakie playing together was made in O'Connor's in 1974. Simply titled 'The Russell Family of Doolin, County Clare,' it includes tunes by them all and songs by Micho. It's a classic recording with excellent sleeve notes by Muiris Ó Rócháin. The three Russell brothers rarely played together after that.

As Irish music became popular in Europe, Micho traveled extensively there, delighting audiences with his manner and his music. Many were enchanted enough to make the pilgrimage back to Doolin and experience where he came from. As backpackers traipsed into O'Connor's in search of culture, Pakie wondered aloud,

"Where are all the people comin' out of?"

THE LIFE AND TIMES of the Russells go hand and hand with the fate and fortunes of Irish music and dance. The brothers saw both sides: the near death of the folk art, seen by some as primitive and irrelevant; and the slow recovery, nursed by people who recognised what was precious and vital to our culture. An Ireland without traditional music is inconceivable today, but in the 1950s, such a place was in the making. It is a testimony to the heart and spirit of the Russells and their peers that the music survived.

Micho Russell
(1915-1994)

Eldest of the Russell Brothers, Micho was a big man with a unique presence and an open heart. Playing the whistle since his early teens, he had a simplicity in his music that gave it a pure and happy soul. To Micho, tunes came with a story and a relevance, and every piece of music had a bit of history or folklore: they were all connected in his world. He gave his music freely and collector Breandán Breathnach gathered hundreds of tunes from him.

A farmer all of his life, Micho was fifty years old before he set foot on a concert stage. That was the first time he visited Dublin. Next it was London. Then Belgium and France. After that he went to Germany a few times. And then it was America. With his cap shoved back on his head, burly body and round face, Micho became the senior statesman of Irish traditional music. By 1990 he had traveled worldwide, playing music, singing songs, giving workshops and relating nuggets of folklore. Apart from a few bits of clothing he picked up here and there, and the few foreign words he had, the world made no change on him whatsoever. He took it all in his easy-going stride. To Micho, nowhere else in the world had the magic of Doolin.

Traditional musicians who were with Micho on the 'Irish Folk Festival Tour' of Germany in the mid-70s recall how he would bring the house down with his introductions, tunes and songs. Micho spoke to the audience the same as he'd speak to one in Ennistymon. Introducing a jig named 'The Cow that ate the Blanket', he explained that cows were sometimes afflicted with a disease that caused them to eat clothes, shirts, vests, socks etc. Therefore, he would not be surprised if a big cow ate a blanket. Then he played the tune on the flute, two feet tapping happily.

At the end of each concert on the 'Folk Festival Tour', all the musicians came on stage for a big jam. Micho was invariably the last on deck; he'd have been chatting to fans in the hall or having a cup of tea in the dressing room. When he eventually strolled on stage, the audience got on their feet and clapped and cheered. He was the star of the show.

Micho was a regular Sunday Mass-goer and on tour it was important for him to know where he could attend the Sunday service. It was also important to him to be able to send money home and he always enlisted the help of a trustworthy fellow musician to help him with this. He kept track of all his transactions in a small blue notebook, where he also wrote pieces of folklore and bits of tunes that came into his head.

Travelling to strange places never fazed Micho. He had a serenity about him that everything would turn out fine. In ways, he was guided by a star, and even when he got lost, there was no panic and he went with the flow until he was found. Micho had his own Buddha nature. There wasn't a gram of badness in the man.

Being alone with Micho for a while was to catch a glimpse of the world in his view, a world-view from an older time, when Irish was spoken and sense was made of life's happenings through old sayings, proverbs, songs, stories and tunes. Séamus Ennis noted the following about another Doolin man:

"Darby Griffy comes from the old life, and I thought when he left me that I had returned into the world in which you and I live today."

Micho could have the same effect on people. His was the same world that had fed the Irish Literary Renaissance. Yeats, Lady Gregory, Synge and their friends had come across it, albeit from a reserved distance.

Teaching the whistle at the annual Willie Clancy Summer School in nearby Miltown Malbay was a highpoint of Micho's year: passing on a traditional art and meeting old friends like Martin Talty, Bobby Casey, Joe Ryan, John Kelly and P. Joe Hayes. He'd be out every night at sessions and was always given a seat of honor.

BASED ON HIS CONCERTS, Micho figured that people were also interested in the stories and folklore attached to his music. He began thinking about putting a collection of tunes and folklore together and in 1980 he self-published a 32-page booklet called 'The Piper's Chair,' with the help of Americans Barbara Wygol and Jenny Loui. In the introduction, there is a sense of how important Micho thought preserving tunes and stories was. He had the same urgent mission as the storytellers who came to Seamus Delargy fifty years earlier. About his way of playing, Micho wrote:

> I'd be trying to make tunes out of the blue, play them different than anybody. I, myself, was more of a music maker...so you could really say these tunes are composed by myself because they're done to my way of thinking.

This is what made Micho's music unique. And it was impossible to separate the man from his music. His tunes had a vibe of their own and most traditional musicians have at least one of Micho's pieces in their repertoire.

Micho sold his booklets at concerts and brought them to local shops, bookshops and music shops around Ireland. In his own way he became an entrepreneur and published 'The Piper's Chair No. 2' in 1984. An updated edition of No. 2 was later published in New York with new photos and a foreword, *The Whistling Ambassador*, by Dennis C. Winter.

As the years rolled on, Micho continued to tour worldwide, though he complained sometimes of weariness. He was a much sought after performer and now wore shirt and tie, jacket or suit and new cap on stage. He made the look his own, it was as Doolin as his music.

IN THE 1990s, Peter O'Neill and I co-produced The San Francisco Celtic Music & Arts Festival. In summer of 1993 I met Micho and he told me he'd like to play at the San Francisco Festival in March 1994 with Charlie Piggott the melodeon player. We agreed on terms and worked from there. On February 13, 1994, I called Micho at his home and finalized a few details about flights and accommodation. He was in good form and looking forward to the trip, talking about other musicians on the bill. The following Sunday, February 20, Seán O'Connor called me with the news of Micho's death. It seemed bizarre and shocking.

Micho and Charlie Piggott were scheduled to play at the Festival on Sunday, March 6 at 3:30pm. For that slot, we decided instead to do a tribute to Micho and play tunes from his repertoire. Charlie was there, as well as Micho's old friend Mick Moloney, Martin Hayes and I. We were joined by mandola player Fergus Feeley and guitarist Paul Kotapish. There was an empty chair for Micho, and somehow his spirit crept up on us and the music took on Micho's pace and rhythm: 'Garret Barry's', 'The Heather Breeze' and 'Sportin' Nell'. 'Peaitsín's Jig', 'The Little Black Pig' and 'The Walls of Liscarroll'. Rootsy music, with the smell of the meadow and a taste of the sea. Micho was with us alright, it was a session of tunes that stands bright as candles at a shrine.

THE FOLLOWING NARRATIVE is based on our conversations from the 1970s and early '80s, stitched together to provide insight into his music, life and times. As Irish music collector Breandán Breathnach wrote;

"Quiet, patient, light-hearted, Micho is prodigal with his music."

And so he was with his memories and stories too.

My grandmother's people were Flanagans and them Flanagans were train-bearers to the Kings of Connaught. Somehow, they had to leave Connaught and a Flanagan man and his three sons and their families came this way with three horses. The father said they'd settle where the horses stopped and one of them halted below here in Luogh, so one family of Flanagans settled there. The next one stopped beyond in *Bárr Trá* above Lahinch and another family stayed there. The third one stopped below in Cloonanaha and there's Flanagans there still. All them Flanagans were very musical and that's where my father got it. My mother was a Moloney and they had a lot of music too. She played the concertina and was always singing around the house. So our music came from the Flanagans and the Moloneys.

There was three families of Moloneys around here and they were all related. My mother was one of them Moloney families. The oldest man of them all was called The Captain, he was sort of the boss. He used to play a flute and he had a lovely slow style, kinda dreamy. All his sons and daughters played mouth-organs, Jew's harps, concertinas and whistles. Michael was good on the concertina and his brother Paddy Seán played a *Trumpa* (the Jew's harp) and the mouth organ and he was good too. When the Captain and themselves played together, they were so good that dancers used to call them 'Moloney's Jig'.

MICHO RUSSELL

Paddy Seán went to America. The fare was only a few pounds, there was a kinda cheap emigration at the time. He was very sad on the boat, he knew no one and no one was talking to him. So, whatever came over him, didn't he take out a mouth organ and started to play a tune on the deck. There was a German and his family on board and they thought this music was great so didn't they bring him up into the first-class floor of the boat and he had a great time altogether. The German had a big brewery in America and he gave Paddy Seán a good job when they got there.

My father, Aughty Russell, had four brothers. John went to America and never came back. Michael was a teacher below in Liscannor and I met a Christian Brother one time and he said my uncle was a great teacher and a great scholar. That's where brother Pakie, the Lord have mercy on him, got the learning. My uncle Thomas was killed in the battle of Mons in the Great War, and when I was in France one time I went to see his grave. Murt was another uncle and a great dancer, he worked over around the Ballyvaughan side but used to come here for Christmas. My father, God rest him, was a lovely lilter and he had a lot of tunes and a lot of old songs. He played the whistle a bit as well and had a few tunes on the concertina, but 'twas mostly songs that I learned off him. A great song of his was *'Bímid ag ól go Maidin'*—'We'll be drinkin' 'till mor-nan.'

In the winter-time himself and a few more men used to go to a house in Doonagore where they spoke Irish all night and told old stories that went back hundreds of years. My mother had Irish too, but my father and herself only spoke it when they didn't want us to know what they were saying. There was no great encouragement for talking it at the time and only the old people spoke it when they got together.

Old Luogh house looking out on the Aran Islands

THE FIRST MUSICIAN I remember apart from my mother and father, was a fiddler and dancin' teacher called Hennessy. He came around to the houses looking for learners and used to play the fiddle and dance at the same time. I thought he was great.

I was still in school when I went to my first dance, a goin' away dance for a neighbour. I was about ten, I'd say, I was only there for the excitement, watching the people and listening to the music. All the local musicians were there—The Captain, Stepheneen Hardy, Pádraig Flanagan and a man from Moymore called Ronan who played a flute. Someone said he made it himself out of the barrel of a gun and he could knock a grand sweet sound from it. There was a man there playing the tin whistle and 'twas him I was mostly listenin' to. He had a lovely way of playin' and it looked kinda simple to me. So anyway, out in the night didn't the teacher arrive into the house and myself and another young lad hid under the table. The musicians were sittin' on chairs above on the table and 'twas like bein' inside in a big drum with all the tapping of the feet.

MY FATHER, the Lord have mercy on the man, bought me a Clarke's tin whistle one day we were at a fair in Ennistymon. Linnanes used to sell 'em and they cost six pence. They used to sell another lovely whistle called a Tosca, but you never see any of 'em at all now. I s'pose I was ten or eleven years old at the time. So, on the way home anyways, the heifer my father bought at the fair broke away from us and went in over the wall below near Liscannor. I went after her and got her out on the road, but 'twas then I discovered the whistle was gone outa my pocket. I went back lookin' for it, but if I was there yet, I couldn't find it. 'Twas a bad start. Anyways, a few months after, I got another one and our neighbour and cousin, Pádraig (Sober) Flanagan, showed me how to play the scale. He had great patience with me. By ear I was learning for a good start and then we started learning music at school. So, one day the teacher—Tim Sexton from The Blessed Well—he asked me how many notes was there in the scale. So I said six, d'you see I was thinking of the six holes in the whistle.

"Are you blind!" Said he, banging on the blackboard, "there's eight notes in the scale."

That didn't make any sense at all to me. I couldn't make head nor tail of it at all, at all. It started me out on the wrong foot altogether. Only for Flanagan I'd have given up. 'Twas years before I got the hang of it. I had tunes in my head alright, but I couldn't get them out of the whistle. I couldn't understand the meaning of a tune at all.

After I finished with school I worked at home. The farm was small and the land wasn't great, mostly rough and damp. We just kept a cow and pig and a few hens like most other places around, just enough to keep ourselves goin'. There was no point in keepin' any more because that time there was little money in farming. You'd get nothin' for a calf that time. But we planted spuds and cabbage and turnips and sowed oats. My father used to fish from the shore below and my mother would cure the fish, mackerel, ling and the likes. She used to salt them and they were lovely. We kept them in a big barrel. All the families along this coast here used to fish and cure the catch for the winter. We had a bit of a quarry over in Luogh but there wasn't any great demand for stone back then, there was no one buildin' anythin'. In a way, we were luckier than most because we'd a horse and cart. A horse was worth a fortune then and I was able to work for neighbours, drawin' home turf and stones or whatever was needed. My mother was great around the house and she used to make clothes and was a good baker and a cook. And then my father died and I had to kinda take charge of things.

In them days there was the world of music around here. There was an awful lot of old flute-players and concertina players, but only a few whistle-players and fiddlers. Thady Killoughery was the only piper and he usen't to play outside the house. That time, musicians were kinda judged on how they played for dancers. The pace and the rhythm was important. I remember one night beyond at a house dance in Ballycotton a row started between dancers and musicians because of the speed of the set. Dancers could be very hard on musicians.

The best musicians in these parts to play for dancers were Pádraig Flanagan and Stepheneen Hardy. Flanagan was a famous concertina player and when he was playin' at a house dance there wouldn't be room to stir. He was the first player I got tunes from outside of my mother and father. 'Tis no known to God all the tunes he had and all class of stories. He was a great *Ireeshin*. When a dance would be winding up he might start a story that could go on for an hour or two.

Hardy was a great fiddler but the poor devil was given to drink. We were gamblin' a calf in our house the night Stepheneen died below in Ennistymon Hospital. We heard the news in the mornin'. Some people said they heard his fiddle playin' in a couple of different places the night he died. 'Twas very strange.

The old people were great entertainers. I loved to listen to them, especially if they had a few drinks taken. Then they would start singin' songs that went back hundreds and hundreds of years, different kinda songs than you'd hear anymore. 'Twas kinda like church music, but older again than that. I heard later that kind of singing was called a lay and was well over a thousand years old. My father had bits and pieces of a few of them kinda songs. They were about the Fianna and Diarmuid and Grainne. Diarmuid used to fish from the strand below at *Trá Bheag Diarmuide*, near where the Piper's Chair is. That must be two thousand years ago because the Fianna were here around the time of Our Lord.

THERE WAS A LOT of good singers around here and I growin' up. The old people sang mostly in Irish and they had lovely songs—'Styke' Donoghue, Dean Hynes and the Davoren brothers, 'Sober', Jerome and Thomas Connole and others. I learned a lot of songs from them and from my father, God rest him. The Connoles had a lot of Fenian songs too, songs like 'Convict 95' that you don't hear at all now. I didn't sing much when I was young, I was classa shy or somethin'. 'Tis only in the last twenty years or so that I started to sing. My two sisters were great singers, but they didn't sing much in public. They might sing a bit at a Swarie or a house dance or something. Some of the songs I have, I changed the air a bit to suit the words.

In them days too, good instruments were very hard to get. They used to make flutes from bamboo but a lot of the time they weren't too good. They usen't be holed right and they'd be all out of tune and everything. A man from Moymore by the name of Darcy came back from America and brought home a lovely timber flute. He knocked a great sound out of it and played the best flute music I ever heard. That's when I thought I'd learn the flute. My uncle John Moloney brought me home a flute from America and I took it up. Paddy Killoughery was playing flute at the time and I used to go over to him on the Sundays. He was great on the flute and I don't know in the world why he ever gave it up.

There was a lot of music in Paddy's family, 'twas from a relation of his, a man by the name of Martin 'Tarbert' Killoughery that I got that tune 'The Piper's Chair'. There's a stone chair in a field down near the shore and that's where the tune got its name. The chair is shaped just right for a piper and I often sat and played in it myself. 'Tis a heavy chair and a man by the name of 'Sutach' McMahon could lift it up to his waist.

MICHO OUTSIDE JAMSIE CAOILTE'S COTTAGE, FISHERSTREET 1950'S

There's a bit of history connected with the Piper's Chair. When she was young, Martin Killoughry's mother used to go over to that spot for some sort of an entertainment they used to have long ago, I'm thinkin' nearly two hundred years ago. It happened at a certain time of the year, I'm thinkin' it was around May Day, but I'm not so sure because it happened so far back that nobody remembers when.

Anyway, pipers came from all over the country and sat in the stone chair and played for dancers. A special kind of dance was done under three tall poles that were tied together at the top, I'm thinking the dance was called a '*báire*'. Anyway, couples danced in bare-feet, around and in between the poles. So it seems, that whatever man put money in the piper's cap, he could invite a lady to dance. They'd carry on until another man gave the piper more money. And so it went on like that and the lady who got the most dances was given some kinda ribbon or flowers or something as a prize. She was what they called *Banríon an Bháire* (Queen of the Báire). But whatever happened one day, there was a big row when the music stopped and a piper was caught and thrown out into the sea. The poor man was drowned and I'm thinkin'

THE PIPER'S CHAIR

that finished the dancing at the Piper's Chair.

In the field where that Piper's Chair is there's lovely places on the shore. They've grand Irish names like *Poll na Gall, Poll na Mangach, Sruthain na Geata,* and *Trá Beag Diarmauide*. Then there's the *Cingire* and a big strand then like the head of a man. There's the *Dreamaire, Aill na Fiach,* and *Trá Lathan* and several names like that. All these places had history attached to them, and that's all lost now. But 'tis no known to God how old that tune 'The Piper's Chair' is. I played it for Breandán Breathnach and he told me that a man by the name of Petrie collected a version of it from an old fisherman in Kilrush a few hundred years ago. The name the fisherman had for it was 'The Catholic Boy'.

I WAS ABOUT TWENTY when I started playing for dances. I wasn't much good and used to leave bits out of tunes and everythin'. But that time there was so many playin' that you wouldn't be noticed. Then somehow, I got the hang of it all of a sudden and I was off. Paddy Killoughery and myself played a lot together and then when Pakie started on the concertina he used to come with with us too. People used to come lookin' for us to play for dances. Pakie had a very lively way of playing and my way of playing was more or less to sweeten up the music with the flute, not goin' before it. I was always more or less what they call a 'second fiddle.' I never could lead a tune at all, at all. So we more or less let Pakie lead and Paddy would come up even with him on the fiddle. I used sweeten it up then with the flute after them. That's what was making it nice.

One Sunday before the last big war, Paddy Killoughery and myself went to a *feis* down in Dunsallagh, below Miltown Malbay. 'Twas held out in a big field and the competitions were on a stage. I'm thinkin' that was 1935 or '6. Paddy and myself were in for the flute competition. The first one to play was Martin Talty and then Paddy. I was next and I started with a reel, 'The Ashplant.' As soon as I did, two dogs appeared out of nowhere and started fightin' in the middle of the field and everyone was looking at them and nobody was listening to me. But I played on and got first prize, however it happened.

After the competition Martin Talty introduced Paddy and myself to Willie Clancy and Bobby Casey. 'Twas the first time we met them and we all went off to some pub and had a great session of music. Paddy wasn't long playin' the fiddle and he had it with him. He broke a string out in the night and Bobby Casey fixed it with a knot. We had great steam and didn't get home 'til the following day. We were walkin', and there was an old man from this side with us, Seán MacMathúna. He was another great *Irisheen* and must have been seventy years old at the time. He sang old songs in Irish and told stories the whole way home and wouldn't let us sit down for a rest or anythin' in case we fell asleep. He was a great scholar and used to collect for the Folklore Department in Dublin.

'Twas around that time I'm thinkin' that I heard Johnny Doran the piper at a fair in Ennistymon. He had a big crowd around him and every time he changed into a different tune a huge cheer went up. I never heard anything like the music he played or saw anyone playing like him. He used to play standing up, with his left leg on a timber box. I don't know how he could do it and play reels so fast. I heard him play 'Lord Gordon's' and 'Colonel Frazer's'. 'Twas great, an' farmers dancin' around half-drunk and shoutin' "round the house and mind the dresser!" I remember a man giving him a pint of porter from a pub when he was finished and people tossing money into the timber box. He was a great piper, God be good to him.

Apart from goin' to Lisdoonvarna or Ennistymon or maybe Lahinch, we usen't to stir far from Doolin that time. I cycled to Ennis a few times to *feises* and competitions. You'd hardly ever see a car up this side of the country, except maybe on a Sunday with some visitor or other. Or maybe some crowd staying inside in Lisdoonvarna might pass over the road on their way to the Cliffs of Moher. Compared to today, the place looked awful quiet altogether. And yet in those years before the war, there was dances four an' five nights of the week around here. Every night we'd be gone.

'Twasn't too bad when there was just myself, but when Pakie and Gussie started movin' out, my mother, God rest her, took a bit of a set on the music. She used to get a bit nervous that we weren't lookin' after things at home. 'Twasn't easy bein' out all night and have to face into a day's work in the morn. Often the bed wouldn't be warm 'til you'd be out of it again.

But we worked hard as well. Turf had to be cut and hay saved, we had to put down spuds and sow cabbage and oats. I worked at all sorts of jobs and Pakie and Gussie were workin' the quarry and doin' bits of stonework here and there. Gussie used to go down along the shore fishin' and gatherin' barnacks and periwinkles in the summer. We were very busy with everything. Then during the war, Pakie and Gussie got jobs in the Doolin mines. There was a lot more to be done at home then, so it wasn't easy at all.

A lot of people started going to England before the war. There was work there and it was easier and cheaper to get there than America. That time you'd be in London in a day but sure 'twould take you a couple of weeks to get to America. At Christmas we might get a parcel or a bit of money from relations in America, but the war kinda stopped that.

The big thing people used to bring back from America that time was the gramophone. 'Twas a great novelty in the beginning, but the people couldn't dance to the music. Too fast. When we heard players like Michael Coleman on the gramophone records, we couldn't believe it at all. You see, that time people only knew the music around their own place. Some players changed their way of playin' altogether

MICHO RUSSELL AND FRIEND IN O'CONNOR'S, 1970

after hearin' these records. They thought, you see, if it was on a gramophone record from America it must be the right way. Before that they played slower.

THE WAR DIDN'T AFFECT US much up around here apart from the rationing. Pakie and Gussie joined the LDF (Local Defense Force) and they used to be off trainin' an' drillin' on the Sundays. I never drilled or trained myself. So, one night a Guard by the name of Irvine called to the house and he was very excited. He said there was a submarine out beyond Moher and there was going to be an invasion. He wanted the lads to come down to the shore with him, but Pakie said we had a cow calving and they'd be down by 'n by. So, they never went down but anyways nothin' happened, there was no invasion. I'm thinkin' that finished Gussie and Pakie with the LDF.

Of course the Doolin mines were operatin' and that brought a good deal of work to the area. There wasn't so much emigration then and people had a bit of money so things weren't too bad. Often wrack used to be washed up on the shore after the storms and that was a godsend—bales of rubber and big pieces of timber. A small barrel of brandy was washed up below in *Trá Lathan* one time and there was dancin' for a week after it. The house dances were still goin' on but then dance halls began to open and the younger people started goin' to them.

Around that time too, the priests took bit of a set on the country dances. They made out there was a lot of blaggardin' at the dances and gave sermons against them at Mass and everything. Some law was passed against the house dances, and between priests and Guards, that finished the whole thing. By the time the war was over, the big house dances were gettin' seldom. The céilí bands were startin' off and most of the dances were in halls in towns and villages. The country was quiet.

The mines closed down then and work was scarce so people had to go to England again. There was a lot of work there and a good many from around here left. Things got very quiet, there wasn't much happenin' at all. At night people played cards and visited certain houses for a chat and that kinda thing but I'm afraid there wasn't much music at all.

THE PIPER'S CHAIR

The young crowd weren't that interested in learnin' to play it. The wireless was comin' in at that time too so maybe that had some effect on it.

SÉAMUS ENNIS was the first one to collect music from us. He came around here on a bicycle just after the war. I'm thinkin he was workin' for the folklore people in Dublin at the time. He wrote down tunes from Pakie. A few years later I remember he came up to the house with Cuckoo O'Brien one fine summer's day. Pakie and Gussie and myself were workin' in the haggard and we were talkin' to them. So, my mother came out of the house to see who we were talkin' to and the next thing Cuckoo and herself had an argument in Irish. She got right vexed with him and cried him out and called him all the names under the sun.

Gussie went off down to the shore and Séamus Ennis just stood there pretending nothin' was wrong. He was right droll and had a great ear for music. He had no recorder, just a pen and paper and he could take a tune down in a couple of go's. Pakie and myself played for him and I gave him 'Carty's Reel'. It came from a Galway piper who used to come to the Pattern Day in Inisheer every year, and had great tunes, different altogether to the music around here. So, a flute player from here called Carty brought the tune back but he was missing a small part of it. I made a bit up for it and it fitted grand. It took Séamus about a half-an-hour to write down my part. He got right mad altogether because he couldn't get the hang of it. And I don't know why because it's very simple.

CARTY'S REEL

curraghs leaving Inisheer and heading for Doolin. The people would be coming in to go down to the Blessed Well, near Liscannor. I remember seeing the long black cars coming from Connaught

There's a tune called 'Loch na Gar' that I played for Séamus Ennis and he sang with it; he had a version he heard in Scotland.

The same tune caused an argument between two brothers who lived below in Liscannor long 'go. They were called the Diddler and the Brónach and one night they fell out over how the tune should be played. So, the only person they knew who had it right was Murty Flanagan beyond in *Barr Trá*, above Lahinch. Anyway, the Diddler and the Brónach said they'd go over to him. So they put down the curragh and rowed across the bay and the agreement was, that whoever had the tune wrong had to row back home by himself. They got to *Barr Trá* anyway and went up to Flanagan and he listened to the two versions and said the Diddler had the tune the right way. So the Brónach had to row back by himself and on the way home didn't he see *Killstuipheen*, the sunken city and the poor man was dead a short time after.

The Garland weekend used to be a big time for music. It could happen that the Saturday morning would be awful rough altogether, and about one or two o' clock in the day the sea would get as calm as a loch, and we would see a line of

with women in big hats and shawls. The cars were drawn by two big Clydesdale horses walking slowly. They came all the way over from Connaught to the Blessed Well on Garland Saturday, 'twas a famous place. There used to be lovely *sean nós* singing by the Aranachs by the side of the road and music in Murphy's pub and Considine's. People used be dancin' sets in the road and more prayin' and doin' the rounds by the holy well.

After spending the night there, the crowd went down to Lahinch. More used to come from other places and on a fine Garland Sunday there would be at least 20,000 people in the village of Lahinch. One time there used to be horse racin' in the strand but I don't remember that, although my father had a song about a horse that won a great race there. When I first started going to Lahinch on Garland Sunday there used to be dancing on the promenade and music in most of the pubs. I seen Johnny Doran playing there as well. He was over on the promenade and there was a huge crowd around him and a lots of people dancing sets. 'Twas great. Everyone was in great form on Garland Sunday and in older times again I heard them say it was a great time for matchmaking.

Séamus Ennis came back sometime later and recorded us for Radio Éireann. Then a while later, Ciarán MacMathúna recorded us again for Radio Éireann below in O'Connor's. There was a good crowd in it the same night and he came again a couple of times after that. He had us on the radio a lot. My mother didn't know what to make of it, she couldn't believe it at all when neighbours told her we were on the wireless.

By the time I started goin' to the fleadhs in the '50s, people from other parts had heard us on the radio. I'm thinkin' the fleadh cheols made a big difference to the music. People got interested in it again and only for that I'm afraid it could have been gone altogether. The first fleadhs were great. I didn't know there was as many musicians in the country until I started to travel out. Paddy Killoughery and myself went to fleadhs all over Ireland. One time we went to the All Ireland Fleadh in Mullingar and there was awful trouble there. For a finish things got a bit out of hand—not with the musicians at all at all, but a rough ol' crowd that were only there for the drink. There was big rows in the street and everything and in the end they had to call in the army from the Curragh. A man by the name of Slugger O'Grady was in charge of the army and they beat all before them with hurley sticks. So, however it happened Paddy Killoughery got lost and I was a bit worried about him. But anyways, at about three or four o' clock in the morn, I was leavin' some pub or other and who did I see at a street corner but Paddy and another man. They were swoppin' fiddles and playin' tunes. The man that was with him was Martín Byrnes and 'twas the first time I met him. He was great steam and brought us back somewhere and we ended up staying the night there.

When the céilí bands were all the go, I was with one in Lisdoonvarna called the 'Naomh Éanna Céilí Band'. Seán Jordan was in it and Peter Griffin and Jimmy Lysaght the fluteplayer from Ennistymon. Players came in and out of the band and Joe Leary the fiddle player was with us for a start. I'm thinkin that band held for five or six years.

Then we stared 'The Doolin Céilí Band'. Gussie and Pakie were in that band, and Paddy Killoughery and myself. Paddy Mullins from Cahersherkin used to play with us sometimes as well. Michileen Conlon, Willie Beg, Gerald O'Loughlin and Jack Killoughery could be with us too, and maybe Joe Leyden or John Patrick O'Loughlin. We played in a good few places, Doolin had a great name for dancin' so we were popular enough around Inagh, Ennistymon, Ballyvaughan and places. We even went as far as Cooraclare and Ennis. Gerald used to drive and play the drums. I s'pose we played one or two nights a month at the most. But 'twas hard to keep goin', because fellas had work to do at home and go to the bog and cut hay too. And if someone had a cow calving, they wouldn't go with the band. So for a finish we gave it up.

My mother wanted to be near the main road, she was gettin' old, so we started building the new house here. We built it mostly ourselves, apart from the roofin'. When 'twas ready and everything and we were movin' up, Pakie wouldn't come with us and stayed below. We thought he'd be up in a few days, but he stayed below for seven years by himself.

Apart from a few times a year, there wasn't much music in the Doolin pubs. The music was kinda dyin' out when you think of it. The Killougherys, Michileen an' ourselves were the main ones playin' for a finish. Back then there was no visitors much coming around. They were coming to the Cliffs alright and to Lahinch and Lisdoonvarna but they seemed to miss Doolin.

'Twas the 1960s anyway, when visitors started comin' around here. That time as well there was a kind of revival goin' on. The Dubliners and other ballad groups were popular and singin' was a big thing. Younger people started playin' Irish music and somehow or other a lot of them came down here. They liked the music and the set dances in the pubs.

At first they came for the weekends, from Dublin and other parts of the country. Publicans weren't too strict about closin' time then and places used to stay open kinda late. Somehow it seems visitors enjoyed themselves around here. Of course they caused a bit of excitement too and that came out in the music. There were great nights here, parties an'

Micho Russell, Michileen Conlon
and Paddy Killoughery, O'Connor's 1964

everythin'. That brought more people to the place.

Tony MacMahon met me at a fleadh somewhere, and he asked me would I go to Dublin to play at Slattery's in Capel Street. I said I would and so a fella came down to drive me up, his name was Mick Hand and he was a fluteplayer with the 'Castle Céilí Band' in Dublin.

So Mick brought me up anyways and that was my first time in Dublin, and the first sort of a concert I ever played for. I'm thinkin' Tony might have recorded it for the radio. I met Joe Ryan and John Kelly there and Martín Byrnes and we had great steam.

So anyway, Mick or Tony introduced me to a man called Breandán Breathnach. Breandán was collecting music that time for the Department of Education. So, 'twas great that I got to know him and every time I was in Dublin we'd meet and I'd give him ten or twelve tunes. By the time I was finished up with him, I had given him over five hundred tunes.

OTHER MUSICIANS who used to come down to Doolin started asking me to go places. Mick Moloney asked me over to England and that was the first time I ever left Ireland. That was around 1969. Mick was with a ballad group called the 'Johnstons' and they were very good. I couldn't tell my mother where I was goin, she'd have got nervous if she knew I was goin' that far. I didn't think London was much different from Dublin in appearance but I thought the people looked a bit strange at me on the street. The folk clubs were great though, the people were very interested in the music and the songs, a lot of them told me they never heard anything like it ever before. It seems all that kind of culture had died out years before in England. One night I was playin' at a folk club and Christy Moore was in it. The next time I was in England, 'twas a man called George Henderson who brought me over to Newcastle-on-Tyne and I played in a few folk clubs.

When I had started movin' out at all, I was invited to go here and there and to places I never knew much about before. I went to Belgium and France with Tim Lyons. We were there for a couple of weeks and I went to see my uncle's grave in Mons. But that wasn't a great tour because we missed trains and buses to places. One time we got right lost and had to hire a taxi to bring us to the club. So we were drivin' for miles and miles and Tim was tryin' to talk to the driver but he couldn't understand us at all at all. For a finish we got to the concert and the people were leavin' to go home. We made nothing that night.

Another time I went to Germany and Austria with Susan O'Connor and Jimmy Moloney. Susan was playin' the pipes and the whistle and Jimmy was dancin'. I remember we were travellin' for days before we played our first night in Germany. I don't know in the name of God how we managed to get around at all, at all. But people were very good to us and we were never stuck for somewhere to stay or anything. We were playin' in folk clubs mostly and people took a likin' to the music and gave us a great welcome everywhere.

Tony MacMahon brought Pakie and myself to Dublin to go on his television programme, '*Ag Déanamh Ceoil*'. We went to O'Donoghue's afterwards and had a few tunes with John Kelly and Joe Ryan. 'Twas Pakie's first time in Dublin and he couldn't wait to get home.

That was around then that I bought this flute from a man by the name of Paul Davis. 'Tis a right good instrument and the best one I ever had. There's something about it, like it kinda plays by itself. A man from America wanted me to let him bring it to America to use as a model to make ones like it but I didn't want to let it go.

I WON the All Ireland flute competition at Listowel Fleadh in 1973, and met a man there by the name of Carstin

Poor Little Fisherboy

Down in the lowlands a poor boy did wander,
Down in the lowlands a poor boy did roam.
By his friends he was neglected, the boy looked as if rejected,
Ah, the poor little fisherboy is far away from home.

He stood on the beach and around him flowed the waters,
He stood on the beach but alas no father came,
Here I am a stranger, exposed to every danger,
Cried the poor little fisherboy so far away from home.

A lady did see him as she looked through her window,
And into her father's house she desired the boy to go.
The tears came to her eyes as she heard the boy's cries,
For the poor little fisherboy so far away from home.

She begged from her father for him some employment,
She begged from her father not to let the boy to go.
Said the father now don't grieve me,
this little boy will never leave me,
Poor lad I will relieve you, so far away from home."

'Tis many the days he laboured for his noble master,
'Tis many the days he laboured until he became a man,
Now he tells a stranger of the hardships and the danger,
Of a poor little fisherboy so far away from home.

Micho learned this song from Thomas Connole. Sung to the air of *All Around My Hat I Will Wear a Green Ribbon*.

Lindos. He wanted Pakie and myself to go to Germany the following year with the Furey Brothers. He was goin' to drive over to Doolin and bring us back with him. So, the two of us were going to travel but something stopped Pakie at the last minute. He never went. I went on my own and joined up with Finbar and Eddie Furey.

The bit of money from the music came in handy and we were able to do bits around the house. Pakie and Gussie and myself were asked to several places but they never wanted to go. We'd never have made the record if the crowd hadn't done it below in O'Connor's. And when the record came out we were invited to go to a lot of places, in Ireland and out foreign too. But somehow or other, Pakie and Gussie had no interest in stirrin' out, so I went on my own. However it happened, but the record wasn't a great deal. We got a hundred pounds between the three of us and 5% in royalties after that. It seems the company got broke and we never got any more money out of it. I saw it for sale in America afterwards.

I was on the Irish Folk Festival Tour in Germany a good few times. That was a big tour, The Fureys, Clannad, De Danann, Noel Hill, Tony Linnane and all them used to be on it as well. We used to travel around in a big bus and we played a good lot in universities and big concert halls. I noticed that every year the crowds comin' to hear us were gettin' bigger an' bigger and I'd meet people who had been in Doolin. The Irish music was more popular in Germany than 'twas in some places in Ireland. I was in Denmark,

Sweden and Norway, Holland, Switzerland, Brittany and all these classa places. I always had a great time anywhere I went, 'twas a kinda holiday playin' music and singin'.

Mick Moloney invited me over to America for the Bi-Centennial Festival (1976). There was a good crowd from Clare invited, Ollie Conway from Mullagh was in it and a few dancers. On the plane over to New York we were playin' music an' singin' and everything and 'twas great steam. Someone said what about dancin' a set and we all went down to the back of the aeroplane where there was a bit of room and the Mullagh crowd danced a half-set. Imagine that, above in the sky an' they batterin' and shoutin' an' everythin'. The pilot came down to see what all the racket was about, but no one took any notice of him. Most of the concerts we played for the Bi-Centennial were outside in the open air and 'twas roastin' hot. I thought I'd never stick it, the sweat would be pourin' off you before you'd go on the stage at all. Mick Moloney was organising the Irish music end of it and he was very good to us. We were in Fort Dodge, Baltimore, Philadelphia, Chicago and Washington.

I was always very lucky travelling around, but it's hard, not so easy at all. You have to be prepared to lose sleep and all that. I used to be very nervous at first, afraid that I'd get lost or lose my seat in a train or a plane somewhere out foreign. But I always managed to get by and come home safe.

Doolin

I MET TWO PROFESSORS from Germany one night in Doolin. So I asked them what made Irish music popular in Germany. So the answer they made me was, that when the young German teenagers heard Irish music first they thought it was just for clapping to, just a kind of entertainment for the time being. But then the older ones, especially the students and teachers started recording the music and brought it home to listen to and study it. They found it was a lot more then entertainment, something much different altogether—it had something to do with culture and folklore and art and literature. They had nothing like it themselves because all their culture got lost in the war. They kind of adopted the Irish in place of their own. It all started in the universities. Two professors told me that. They said this folklore and culture of ours was a gift.

I'm thinking myself that it should be brought very strongly into the education because people don't know about it at all. The children should know about it because 'tis goin' fast. I'd like if every player stuck to their own parish and the way the old people played. I think music makes a place happier somehow. It must be good for people or something.

MICHO AND DOLLY MCMAHON,
LISDOONVARNA FESTIVAL, 1979

PAKIE RUSSELL
(1920 - 1977)

MUSICIAN, STORYTELLER, SINGER and stonemason, Pakie Russell was the youngest of the brothers. He had a deep intelligence and unbridled imagination, coupled with a sense of fun and the absurd. Though he rarely moved very far from Doolin, he had a remarkable knowledge and insights to life and the outside world. As Paddy Pharaic Mhichil Shannon said, "Pakie could throw a lot of light on things."

He finished school in the mid-1930s and went to work in the family quarry with his brother Gussie. In Doolin, English was becoming the daily language and farm machinery was replacing manual labor. The *meitheal* and the sweet Irish language, fabric of the old community were fraying. While Pakie was learning how to quarry, American anthropologist Conrad Arensberg was studying the disappearing ways of life the townland of Luogh.

Micho said:

Pakie was very smart and great at school an' everythin' but my mother thought he was classa delicate and kept him at home after he finished in the national school. I'm thinkin' he could have gone further. He went workin' in the quarry with Gussie later on and became a stonemason. He was good too, and had a great feel for stone and buildin'. Only there wasn't much demand for that sort of work around here then.

Pakie learned an awful lot from the old people. Of course he had great Irish, somehow he had a bigger interest in it than the rest of us. He used to go over to Peaitsín Flanagan's house in the nights and be there till all hours, listenin' to stories and talk about long ago. He liked visitin' the old people and they had great time for him.

ONE OF PAKIE'S haunts was Anthony Moloney's house near the bridge in Fisherstreet. Moloney's was a *teach ragairne*, a gathering house for the old Irish speakers around Doolin. It was in Moloney's that Seamus Delargy met Stiofán Úa Ealaoire in December 1929. Séamus Ennis visited Moloney's in September 1945 and during a happy night there with the old tradition-bearers, he noted: "A young man took a whistle from his pocket and played some tunes for us…"

The young man was Pakie, although Ennis would not discover his name for a few days. Being in the company of old *Irisheens* like Styke Donoghue and Peaitsín Flanagan was an indication of where Pakie's interest lay. He was a tradition-bearer in the making, tuning into the world of the old people, and soaking up their art and glory. Ennis came across him again on the following Sunday evening, when he went for a walk after his dinner at Gertie Murphy's in Ballaghaline.

> (I heard) gentle, fine music and I saw five or six lads lying on their stomachs on the roof of the swimmers' bathing boxes. I settled down beside them and there were two people beneath us in one of the boxes. They were playing tin whistles as sweetly as you could wish to hear. One of them was Pat Russell (c. 24), the same man who had the tin whistle at *O' Maoldhomhnaigh's* (Moloney's) house on Friday night. It was not long before he knew I was there and I was invited down to play. I was smoking my pipe and I preferred to continue to listen and so I asked them to keep playing. They then played a nice jig that I did not know and I went down to them in a flash to write it from them. I believe I wrote around six tunes from them in the two hours of music that followed and Pat told me that he had heard them from his mother's lilting. Here I am again, getting the most interesting information on the day of my departure!
>
> I said goodbye to Pat and to the happy young men who had gathered there. I did not notice if the visitors around had come to listen to the inspirational whistle music in the course of the afternoon, but these young lads were brilliant.[1]

While his whistle playing clearly impressed Seamus Ennis, Pakie's main instrument was the concertina. His mother played one and he took a liking to it and learned from her. According to Micho, he practiced by himself for years and never brought the concertina outside the house:

> He never pretended to anyone outside the house that he was learnin'. Pakie was at it a few years by the time Pádraig Flanagan heard about it, and he

asked him over one Sunday evenin' to play a couple of tunes. When Flanagan heard him playing, the eyes nearly jumped out of his head. He couldn't believe Pakie was doing the things he was hearin' from the concertina. He said he couldn't teach him anything, and that he had it all learned. That was the first time Pakie played outside our own house, he was about twenty at the time. After that, Flanagan kinda let him take over from him.

PAKIE WORKED in the mines until his mother thought it was interfering with his health and persuaded him to quit. It was back to the quarry by day and music by night. The mines were thriving and Doolin was hopping with house dances. The popular local combo became Pakie on concertina, Micho on concert flute and Paddy Killoughery on fiddle. They were playing for house dances a few times a week and they had some great years of music and sport. Pakie himself was a good set dancer, and Micho said:

> He knew how to play for dancers. He liked to play fast and lively and when he was dancin' himself, 'twas very hard to play for him. He used to do fierce givin' out if the music wasn't the right pace or hadn't the right 'lift'. Sometimes he might get disgusted and leave the floor altogether.

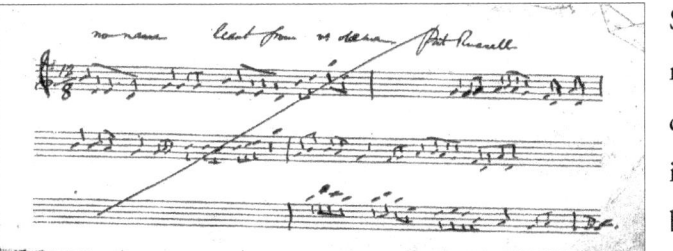
UNTITLED TUNE COLLECTED BY SEAMUS ENNIS FROM PAKIE

SOON AFTER WWII the mines closed, house dancing declined and the able-bodied were emigrating. It was back to hard times. Without dances there was little music and less fun around Doolin; a dwindling population of Irish speakers and the passing of the storytellers meant fewer nights around the cottage fireside. As Pakie approached his thirties, the social life he knew and cherished was fast disappearing. Micho recalled:

> I'm thinkin' he was unhappy when the music in the houses kinda stopped altogether, everyone was goin' away and money was scarce. He used to often talk about goin' to England when things weren't goin' right for him. We had a sister married over there but my mother didn't want him to go because she thought 'twould ruin his health.

Life was quiet and the big events at the turn of the 50s were the visits of Séamus Ennis and Ciarán MacMathúna, who recorded the Russells and other local musicians for Radio Éireann. Unlike Micho, Pakie didn't attend many early fleadhs and never strayed too far from Doolin. Home life was bleak and there could be disagreement between the brothers. Micho said:

Pakie was fierce particular about things gettin' done right. If he thought you were doing somethin' the wrong way, he'd get right disgusted and throw down the fork or the shovel and walk away from the job. He had his own way of thinkin' about a lot of things.

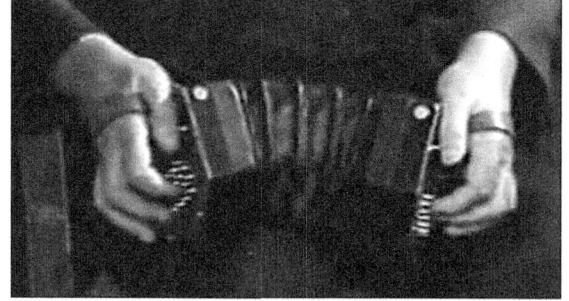
PAKIE'S CONCERTINA

When we moved up here from the old house, he wouldn't come with us and stayed below on his own for six or seven years. Every night he'd be readin and listenin' to foreign stations on the wireless 'till all hours.

Pakie used to say that pension day was the liveliest day in Doolin during the 1950s, when the old *Irisheens* met up for a drink or two in Considine's bar after collecting their funds at the post office. Other than that, there wasn't much laughter or fun. Around this time Pakie was part of the Doolin Céilí Band, and by some accounts he was the *enfant terrible* of the ensemble.

With great relish he used to tell of a massive Swarie that was held near Miltown Malbay in the mid-1950s. A cultural depth charge, it went on for three nights. On the second night, Pakie and Paddy Killoughery turned up for the 'scrap party' with Martin Talty, Willie Clancy and Joe Cuneen, the flute player from Quilty. There were sets danced in the house and more tunes played in the sheds. And there were oceans of drink. Three outhouses were converted into bars and the farmyard and the haggard were packed. What he described was as subversive as a rave. The place was bursting at the seams, and on the third night, members of the Kilfenora céilí band arrived. They took no prisoners and drove it through the roof.

"Jesus," said Pakie, "people were goin' around in circles for weeks after that Swarie."

PAKIE PLUCKED UP COURAGE IN 1959 to enter the senior concertina competition in the Clare county fleadh, which was held that year in neighboring Lisdoonvarna. It was on an August weekend during a scorching spell and the town was packed and uncomfortable. Pakie didn't win the competition and soon left town for O'Connor's. He was nursing his sorrows when a carload of old friends arrived— Séamus Ennis, Willie Clancy, Martin Talty, and Martín Byrnes. Another car brought Ciarán MacMathúna, Seán MacReamoinn and Leo Rowsome. A meeting of like-minded souls, with music, songs and *sean nós* dancing. The waves that session sent out brought more music lovers to Doolin the following day. After that, O'Connor's became a musical mecca and Pakie never entered another fleadh competition.

A few years later, Pakie met Tipperary poet Michael

Coady, who had a holiday music gig in Lisdoonvarna. Michael took a walk to Doolin and stopped at McDermott's in Roadford for a pint. Pakie was the only other drinker in the pub and when he learned Coady was a musician, he asked,

"Did you ever hear tell of the fiddle being played with a swan's feather?"

It was a sentence worthy of Gabriel Garcia Marquez, and Pakie and Michael became lifelong friends.

A BACHELOR LIKE BOTH his brothers, Pakie was about forty then. A good-looking man, he had a twinkle in his eye and a musical way of talking. In rural Irish terms he was still of 'marrying age', but Pakie kept well away from the altar for reasons of his own. He eked out a frugal living between the quarry and subsistence farming, and began to ramble to the pub a bit more frequently. O'Connor's became his main haunt and he brought his music, stories and philosophies with him. Michael Coady was a regular visitor, with his friends Seamus McGrath, Michael Greany and Michael Powell. They were the vanguard, a few years ahead of the stream.

BY THE MID-'60S, most Irish traditional music aficionados had heard of the Russell Brothers via programmes on the radio or by Micho's appearance at fleadhs and concerts around Ireland. The fiftieth anniversary of the Irish Rising in 1966 coincided with a 'ballad boom' and folksongs became popular outside their natural habitat. Folk clubs sprang up in cities. Groups like Sweeney's Men and The Dubliners mixed in tunes with the songs, and jigs and reels seemed contemporary and relevant. There was a search for authentic Irish music and song, away from the crowds and the traffic. Somehow more and more musicians and listeners discovered Doolin. It was heaven—good music, good porter, plenty of banter and dance. Outside you could smell the sea and look at green hills instead of shops and houses. Doolin then was a remote sanctuary.

PAKIE ENLIGHTENING VISITORS, 1960S

WHILE MICHO was the Buddha-like evangelist, Pakie was more the guru who stayed at home and waited for the world to come to him. And it did. The genie was out of the bottle by 1970 and there was a steady stream of visitors coming to Doolin. Pakie had abandoned the stonework, just as it was becoming a popular feature in building.

The last stonework he did was in O'Connor's—external wall facings and the fireplace in the bar. Life was getting merrier and most nights there were tunes in O'Connor's and visitors to spice things up. Pakie played with Willie Beag Shannon (fiddle), Paddy Killoughery (fiddle), Joe Leyden (accordion), and Stevie MacNamara (bodhran). Rory O'Connor played tin whistle from a high stool at the counter and Micho or Gussie might play at the periphery of the session.

Pakie played best for his own people, the Doolin dancers and often encouraged local bar patrons to take to the floor for a half-set. Jamsie Caoilte seldom refused the call, often dancing alone in a long black coat and Wellington boots. His performance was a mix of the Aran Set and *sean nós* dancing, in perfect time, often shaking a cudgel. When Pakie was in form, his playing was lively and fiery with a carefree 'lift'. He seemed to be in a trance, away in another world: eyes widening and bulging, lips pursed in a smile. He stared straight ahead of his music, only breaking to shout at Jamsie, "Confine yourself to the arena!"

Musicians came to pay their respects to Pakie, introduce themselves to him, shake his hand and maybe play a tune together. He had a following, they heard about him through word of mouth, a reel on the radio, the recommendation of a friend. He enjoyed the company and the appreciation. Poets and writers sat and talked with him, he answered professors as he twiddled his thumbs and enlightened them on Brehon law. Few met Pakie Russell who were not impressed by the man and his mysterious store of knowledge.

Pakie's liveliness came through in his concertina playing, and his sensitivity showed in his singing. His rendition of 'The Banks of the Lee' evoked loneliness, and maybe an absence of love. In the chorus he sang '...the Trá on Inisheer' instead of the 'Banks of the Lee', making that song of love and emigration feel very immediate. It was like his own story, in some Irish way.

His speech was unforgettable—a rising and falling melodic voice that bordered on singing. He carried listeners away in a couple of sentences and turned the ordinary into the extraordinary when he told a story, or gave an account of something weird and wonderful that he had come across somewhere. He enchanted with his tales; some were as old as the hills, with new bits

Susan O'Connor, Gerald 'The Count' Barry, Pakie Russell and Michael Sherlock

fitted in; others he made up himself, sprinkling them with bits of Irish or Latin. It was improv storytelling at its best and he was a master of the art. He could silence O'Connor's bar with a tale about a pair of boots he bought at a fair in Ennistymon. Micho said:

> Pakie was a sort of a philosopher and a lot of people used to come to Doolin especially to talk to him about things. They were very interested in what he had to say, and one time I heard him tellin' two professors from the Isle of Man about old stories from there and he surprised the life out of them. They couldn't know how he had that kind of knowledge at all, at all. That was the book learnin' I s'pose. When people met him in Doolin, they used to send him books and newspapers and things like that. He had an awful lot of knowledge altogether.

Pakie was coming to O'Connor's daily by the mid-1970s. He liked to get there in the afternoon, while the pub was quiet and have a few solitary pints sitting in the súgán armchair by the fireplace. Most nights he played a blast of tunes and there was always fun and banter in the bar and a few visitors for colour.

A television crew from the French 3rd National Channel recorded extensive footage of music sessions in O'Connor's in 1973. This is part of the documentary *Ireland: A Nation's Memory* and includes a duet by piper Willie Clancy and Pakie, which would be their last tune together. It was a busy year for Pakie. He traveled to Dublin for the first time and performed with Micho on *Ag Déanamh Ceol*, a programme produced by their friend Tony MacMahon. That summer The Russell Family album was recorded in O'Connor's. Interest in the brothers grew and they received invitations and offers to play at concerts at home and overseas. Pakie and Gussie declined and Micho went off on his own or with a good friend or two. Micho remembers:

> A good lot of people wanted Pakie to travel out foreign to play at festivals and things, but he wasn't interested. Dublin was as far as he went and that was

Martin Howley's Reel— a favourite of Pakie's

only because Tony McMahon asked us to play on the television. Gussie wouldn't come. After I went to Germany the first time, I was tellin' him about all the lovely buildings and the big places and what he said to me was, "You don't have to go two miles from your own door to see the finest buildin' in the world. The Cliffs of Moher beats anything made by the hand of man." I'm thinkin' the only other place we traveled to was *Radio na Gaeltachta* in Connemara to do a program for Seán Bán Breathnach. We stopped in Spiddal and met up with Festy Conlon on the way home.

PAKIE BALKED AT BECOMING anything even remotely like a semi-professional musician. He turned down offer after offer to tour and record, saying that 'someone has to hold the fort.'

Rather than taking the concertina home with him, he left it behind the counter, from where it could be summoned fast as a pint. He was in O'Connor's every day, sitting in the *súgán* armchair by the fireplace, drinking porter and watching life pass by.

Some nights he played, more nights he didn't. There were always people to talk to, and he was a curious listener as well as a great narrator. As the years rolled on, it was here he held court, playing less and less music and complaining about pains in his 'bloody bones.'

As more people came to Doolin, Pakie got uncomfortable. The pubs got crowded and local farmers gave way to day-trippers and hitchhikers in search of the real Ireland. Pakie sat in his *súgán* chair, taking it all with a pinch of philosophy. He complained that teeming crowds kept his old friends away and there were fewer people he could have meaningful conversations with. There was nothing sacred anymore, even his old *súgán* seat which sometimes had been taken by a visitor when he got to the pub.

"You know," he announced one evening, "I'm thinking that tourism could become a form of pollution."

AFTER A SHORT ILLNESS Pakie died in Ennis Hospital on September 4, 1977. His death made the evening news on RTE, something which would have made him smile. Micho said of him:

> Pakie's health was never that great and I'm afraid he didn't look after himself too well. We didn't know at all how bad he was and when he used to complain we didn't take too much notice of him. He passed away very fast. Before he died I went down to see him in Ennis hospital and he told me he had money saved up for his funeral for years. 'Twas hidden in the wall of a small shed beside the house, he had it in a small tin beside a certain stone, so many feet in from the door. He was very proud right up to the last.

REFERENCE

1. *Going to the Well for Water: The Séamus Ennis Field Diary 1942-1946,* Editor, Prof. Ríonach uí Ógáin, Director of the National Folklore Collection, UCD.

Gussie Russell

(1917 - 2004)

FLUTE AND WHISTLE player GUSSIE RUSSELL was integral to Doolin music all his life. Shy compared to his brothers, he shunned the limelight and would often be seated at the edge of music sessions. Rarely did he play alone with Pakie or Micho and was known as 'the quiet brother'. He went to fleadhs but never entered a competition, preferring to play in back-room sessions or at late-night street corners. A frequent visitor to Inisheer, he occasionally turned up at the Galway Races, Spancil Hill and the Fair of Ballinasloe. He was always up for a bit of fun with good friends.

GUSSIE ALSO HAD a wildness about him at times and was a regular party goer in the Doolin heydays. He had a second youth when young flute players Michael and P.J. Hynes, Christy Barry and Anthony Howley came to Doolin in the 1970s. All very good musicians, they brought out the best in him and he was in his element playing with them; when Paddy Killoughery joined in, it must have been just like old times for him.

In later life Gussie bought a Honda 50 motorbike and became a familiar sight on the local roads. A cautious driver, he stayed close to the edge and took his time. He said if he'd known how handy a motorbike was, he'd have gotten one years before.

IN THE SUMMER of 1995 I was renovating an old cottage and Gussie promised me flags for the floors. One July morning I called on him with a car trailer and my teenage sons, Aindrias and Eamon. We drove over to the quarry and Gussie had a bundle of tools neatly wrapped in canvas. He looked at the quarry face and pointed to seams from where water seeped.

"There." He said, "that's where we'll hit."

He instructed the lads how to accurately hit the seam with hammers and chisels and yells of "Hit! Hit!" echoed in the quarry. It was like stepping back centuries to see flags lifted from the bedrock with a groan, and see Gussie trimming them to size without tape or rule. Then he showed us how to 'walk' the flags from the quarry to the trailer.

Before I left Doolin with the load of flag, he told me how best to lay them and to put a few coins under the hearthstone so I'd always have money in the house. He later told me that was the last time he worked the quarry.

The following are pieces from our conversations over the years, put together to give a portrait of Gussie Russell.

PADDY PHARAIC MHICHIL SHANNON AND GUSSIE RUSSELL AT CRUINNIÚ NA MBÁD, KINVARA

I ONLY STARTED PLAYIN' the music so I could go on the 'small mummers' on St. Stephen's Day. I s'pose I started playin' for money. I could only blow a couple of notes on the whistle and 'twas funnin' and foolin' we were mostly. But people were glad to see us comin' all the same and we'd collect a few pennies here and there. A penny to me that time was as good as winning the prize-bonds because money was scarce. You'd be scrapin' money for to buy something for ages and when you got to the shops there was nothin' to buy. The country was very empty in them days.

I found the day awful long an' drawn-out in school. I wasn't much good at the books, I used to want to be down the shore, fishin' or throwin' stones into the sea. When I was young I did a lot of fishin' from the rocks, 'twas a great way to pass the time and be doin' something useful while you were at it. Often when I was fishin' I'd be thinkin of tunes, turnin' them over in my head and tryin' to get them right.

EXCEPT FOR THE DEAR WANS, the whistles they sold in the shops were very bad when I was young. They'd be out of tune with themselves and you couldn't play with anyone. The first half-right whistle I had, I made it myself out of a plant called a *Glorawn*. The *Glorawn* was a strong plant that used to grow in the meadows long 'go. You'd cut the stalk of it and put it into a cock of hay or a reek to season. After a while it turned hard and 'twould be hollow in the inside. You'd clean it out and cut a mouthpiece in it. Then you'd measure out the finger holes and drill them. They weren't great whistles but they did the job. But the *Glorawn* don't grow around here anymore since they started putting the bagged manure on the meadows.

MICHO WAS PLAYIN' a good while before me. I was more interested in singin' for a good start because my father had great ol' songs. He had one that he got from a man from Wilbrook who he met on the train to Ennis. It started like "My wife went away today and I'll ne'r see her no more." I can't remember it, but 'twas awful sad.

OPENING OF DOONAGORE CASTLE, 1974:
GUSSIE RUSSELL (FLUTE) WITH MICHO, SONNY MULLINS (FIDDLE), IAN STEVENSON AND ROBERT CROSBIE (ACCORDION)

My mother lilted and played the concertina at night. I learned tunes from her. But I didn't like to play outside the house. There was too many great players around.

On Sundays, Pakie and myself used to go over to Killoughery's to listen to Paddy and John and Thady playin'. They had great drive for dancin', the best you'd ever hear. We'd be over there for hours. I don't know how they put up with us at all, at all. We had them pestered. I'd have the whistle with me but I wouldn't take it out.

I'LL NEVER FORGET the first night I played for a dance. 'Twas below in Doonagore, a dance for someone home from America. I didn't want to play at all and a crowd of the lads caught me and carried me into the house. They put me sittin' down beside Paddy Killoughery.

"How're you Gussie?" said Paddy, "Take out the whistle and give us a hand."

There was no getting out of it, so I played. After that I didn't do much singing, 'twas more playin' for dances I used to be.

The dances were great steam and we'd be playin' a lot at them. For a while there was dances every night and we were gone from home all the time. My mother took a terrible set on the music then. She put us out workin' no matter how tired we were and we had to go. 'Tis often I sweated beyond in the quarry trying to lift flags out and Pakie sittin' down weak with sleep. Durin' the war I worked in the Doolin mines and I often fell asleep above in the dark leanin' on the shovel. The music had us out every night.

DURIN' THE SUMMER we'd go into Aran on the Saturday if the weather was anyway fine. Often a big crowd would go in, there might be three or four curraghs—Rory O'Connor, Jamsie Caoilte, Paddy Pharaic Mhichil and Thady Killoughery used to go in a lot. It was awful wild inside. The Aran crowd used to go cracked for the music and we'd be up all night for a couple of nights without a bed. 'Twas often lightin' day on Monday morn when we got back to Ballaghaline Pier. I used to go up to work, sweat pourin' off me and I as weak as water.

There was no work much around after the war and things got very quiet. An awful lot of people went to England and the dances got scarce. I was down along the shore a lot because a lot of wrack was washed up. I remember gettin' a great big bale of rubber once and Pakie got nine pounds for it from someone. But 'twas mainly planks and strong ropes that were washed up and he sold them to a man who came around in a small lorry. In some place barrels of brandy were washed up, but a barrel of oil was the most we ever got.

I worked for the County Council for a while. They were doing somethin' with the roads and I was breakin' stones for them. 'Twas hard work but I was glad to get the pay. The quarry was a dead loss in them days and there was no money in farming. Then the house dancin' and the tournaments stopped and there was nothing happenin' much for a good few years.

around here when I was a young lad. The last time I saw that sorta dancin was in Rory Connor's house.

The youngsters around here only started learnin' the music again lately. Micho teaches them and he says there's some great young players risin' up. There's more young people playin' the music now then there ever was. 'Tis great to see it popular again, because for a while, a lot of people thought the music was sorta backward or old-fashioned or something. In some places not so long ago, they thought you'd be half-cracked for playin'. You could even be cleared from a pub for takin' out a whistle. Now 'tis how they'd fill you with drink to play a tune.

'**Twas great** to see the visitors comin' here because they brought a bit of life to the place. 'Twas like long ago with the big parties in Jamsie Caoilte's house after the pubs closed. Often they went on all night and were nearly as good as the old dances. Sometimes they were wilder. There used be foreigners there and I don't know in the name of God what they thought of us at all—Jamsie dancin' in his Wellingtons and he langers with *poitín*. Someone else frying rashers an' sausages on the fire and smoke all over the place.

Other times there used to be parties at Rory Connor's house, especially if there was a crowd in from Aran that would be stayin' the night. The old Aran men had a lovely way of dancin', they didn't do any batterin' like the dancers around here. The Aran people had a softer step, their shoes just rubbin' the floor. They didn't do any high steps and danced kinda slow, sorta like the way the old people danced

Photo credits

P. 68 Seán O'Connor, Fisherstreet, ©

P. 71 © RTE

P. 74 © RTE

P. 75 ©Michael Fitzgerald

P. 77 Seán O'Connor, Fisherstreet

P. 78 ©Peter Laban

P. 80 ©Michael John Glynne, Courtesy Clare Co. Library

P. 84 Seán O'Connor, Fisherstreet

P. 85 unknown

P. 87 © RTE

P.88. ©Michael John Glynne, Courtesy Clare Co. Library

P. 89 Seán O'Connor, Fisherstreet

P. 92 A Nation's Memory

P. 93 ©Michael John Glynne, Courtesy Clare Co. Library

P. 94. Seán O'Connor, Fisherstreet

P. 97 Eugene Lambe

P. 98 Seán O'Connor, Fisherstreet

P. 99 ©Peter Laban

P. 100 ©Michael John Glynne, Courtesy Clare Co. Library

P.101 Eugene Lambe

Russell recordings

The Russell Family of Doolin, County Clare, Micho, Pakie and Gussie Russell. Recorded in O'Connor's Bar, Doolin, January 1974.
Originally released on Topic Records,1975

Under the Cliffs of Moher. Micho Russell. Producer: Pearse Gillmore. Xeric Records.

The Limestone Rock. Micho Russell Producer: Brian O'Rourke. GTD Heritage Recording Co. Ltd, Galway.

Micho Russell of Dunagore Co. Clare. Producer: Neil Wayne. Free Reed.

The Singers and Songs of County Clare from the Carroll Mackenzie Collection includes several songs by Micho and one by Pakie.
See www. clarelibrary.ie

Ireland's Whistling Ambassador - Micho Russell of Doolin, Co. Clare, Producer: Bill Ochs, 1995, The Pennywhistler's Press, NY

Micho Russell Rarities & Old Favorites 1949–1993
Producer: Bill Ochs. 2015, Pennywhistler's Press N.Y.

BOOKS BY MICHO RUSSELL

Russell, Micho. 1980 *The Piper's Chair.* A Collection of tunes, songs and folklore. Ossian Publications.

Russell, Micho. 1986. *The Piper's Chair No. 2* a collection of tunes, songs, and folklore. Photos and foreword by Dennis C. Winter. Canal Press, N.Y.

Russell, Micho. 1988. *The road to Aran: Songs, Folklore and Music of West of Ireland.* Micho Russell, Doolin.

Russell, Micho. 1991. *Micho's Dozen: Traditional songs from the repertoire of Micho Russell, Doolin, Co. Clare.* Introduced and annotated by Tom Munnelly. Ennistymon Festival of Traditional Singing, Co. Clare.

Russell, Micho. 1992. *Music & Folklore of Doonagore - Doolin with Micho Russell.*

OTHER RESOURCES

Coady, Michael. 1996. *The Well of Spring Water: a memoir of Pakie and Micho Russell of Doolin*

Doorty, John. *Out of the Heavens in Showers: Interviews with Micho Russell;* Departures Vol. 1 (1996), New Series: Departures Vol. 2 (1997)

Piggott, Charlie. *Micho Russell, Blooming Meadows: The world of Irish Traditional Musicians;* Vallelly, Fintan; Piggott, Charlie. Townhouse and Countryhouse, Dublin, 1998

Many online resources have recordings of Micho as well as sheet music of his tunes. He's also featured on several YouTube videos, as is Pakie.

Ireland: A Nation's Memory (1973) features Pakie and Gussie playing in an old Doolin session that includes Willie Clancy. http://youtu.be/sUy57dtThzM

A sample of songs and tunes recorded from Micho can be accessed at: www.eddiestack.com/michorussell.html

On location in Lahinch — John and Paddy Killoughery discussing music for *The Riordans* (an RTE soap) with producer Brian MacLochlinn.

An evening with
The Killougherys

IN THE EARLY 1930S, there were regular Sunday afternoon music sessions at Killoughery's house in Ballyfaudeen, just over the Doolin border. The sessions were made up of younger musicians who hadn't yet graduated to playing for house dances. John Killoughery played the whistle, Thady was a piper and Paddy played the flute back then.

The Russell Brothers were regular attendees and each family held the other in high esteem. For the next fifty years both families of brothers would soldier together from house dances and pub sessions to fleadh cheols.

In the early '60s, Paddy Killoughery sometimes came to the Sunday night session in my grandmother's house in Lahinch and my earliest memories of him are from there. He would arrive at the back door with fiddle case and a smile and ask if he was at the right house. His polite manner and gentleness, his double-breasted suits, wide tie and Sunday cap all impressed me as a young child. I would lead him into the session in the sitting room and when my grandmother saw him she used to hail,

"Paddy Killoughery my love!"

He would shake hands with her and each of the other musicians. Chairs would be rearranged and the circle widened. My grandmother would get him a bottle of stout and he'd accept it with a smile and several 'thank yous'. He'd have a sip and then tune the fiddle. My grandmother would begin a tune she knew he liked and the music started. Then it was tune after tune, Flanagan, Killoughery and Russell music, local as the stone.

It's another wet winter's evening in North West Clare and it takes Paddy Killoughery a second or two to recognise me in rain gear, when he answers the door. He shakes my hand and invites me inside. His brother John is sitting by the open fire and we exchange greetings. Paddy piles up the fire and says,

"You can't beat a good blaze on a bad night."

"'Tis true for you," says John, turning his attention to my tape recorder and asking questions about it.

"I fix clocks," he told me.

"Oh God he does," added Paddy, "and he's very good too."

I looked around the dim kitchen and saw eight wag-of-the-wall clocks ticking peacefully in the shadows, each telling a different time. John says he fixed a clock for my grandmother about thirty years ago and the conversation turns to her and the great nights of music they had in her house in Lahinch. Paddy asks me who got her fiddle when she died.

"She was a lovely woman and a sweet player," he says.

"She was," said John. "Many is the tune we played together, the Lord have mercy on her."

PADDY KILLOUGHERY

I open a couple of bottles of Guinness from a six-pack I've brought. We discuss the merits and drawbacks of bottled porter for a while and then we talk about music.

"We played a lot of music with the Russells when we were young," John tells me.

"We did," confirms Paddy, "and they were the best of 'em. Pakie, God love him. He was great."

"He was," says John, "he was a great concertina player and we had tunes that used to suit him. We learned a lot of tunes from Martin Killoughery, a relation of our own who played the concertina. He played an older style, you see, himself and Pádraig Flanagan were a great pair. Two concertinas playin' note for note."

"Oh God they were good," Paddy adds.

"All of us started by playin' whistles and flutes," says John, "we brought that from our uncle, Jim Marrinan who came from Cloonah, Ennistymon. He was a great flute player, you'd stand in the snow to listen to him. He used to play with another flute player called Dinny Brennan and you'd want to be a great judge of music to know there was two players playin'. You'd swear there was only one flute, they had exactly the one note."

"They were very tight," says Paddy, "I used to play the

flute myself when I was young. I learned a lot of it from Jim Marrinan. He was a very sweet player and had lovely tunes. We still play them."

"We do," acknowledges John, "Jim was never recorded. There was no recordin' that time."

"I gave up the flute for the fiddle," Paddy says.

"He did and 'twas a pity too because he was good on it."

"I made my first fiddle out of an orange box."

"It wasn't a bad fiddle."

"'Twas hard to get good instruments when we were startin' out," Paddy said.

"They weren't in it," John adds. "I started playin' when I was fourteen or fifteen and 'twas years before I had a right instrument. My brother Thady was the only one around here with a good instrument. He had a set of pipes he bought from Leo Rowsome in Dublin."

"They cost a fortune," remembers Paddy, "he was putting money away for years for them."

"He was. He was good on them too."

"He gave 'em up early, may the Lord have mercy on him."

"There was no pipers around this side," adds John. "They were down around Miltown alright but Thady was the only one up around here."

"There wasn't many fiddlers here either," says Paddy, "Stepheneen Hardy was the best of them but he died young. He was only started on the pipes."

"'Twas a pity. He was a great player. A genius. He burned himself out."

"'Twas easy to do it that time," recalls Paddy.

"'Twas," agrees John, "you see, that time there was something happening every night."

"There was always something," says Paddy, "dances, Swaries, weddings and everything."

"Musicians were in great demand and we were gone every night. You could be out seven nights a week for the whole week and you wouldn't think about it."

"'Twas great," says Paddy.

"'Twas. I remember to be working beyond around Kilfenora one time and I was eight or nine nights out without seeing a bed. So anyway, this day I cycled over to Doolin to collect a suit of clothes the Tailor Shannon was making for me. On the way back home, I was above on my bicycle goin' down a hill and didn't I fall asleep. The next thing I remember, was wakin' up inside in the bog and the bicycle turned upside down on top of me. Wasn't that bad? After eight nights playin' music without a wink of sleep."

"It would get to you," adds Paddy.

"Of course, there was nothing else for the people to do apart from the dances. There was no radios much up this side of the country until after the war. A few people had gramophones

John (1912-2005) & Paddy (1916-1994)

they got from America alright."

"We played in every village from here to Inagh," says Paddy, "But the best dances were down in Doolin."

"They were," agrees John, "The Doolin crowd understood dancin' and they were good at it. Of course there was great players there too. There was always great music around Doolin, however it was. There was a great welcome for it. Sure, there was music in the pubs below in Doolin when you wouldn't get a tune anywhere else. The Russells were always there, sure."

"The Lord have mercy on Pakie," says Paddy, "he kept the whole thing goin' for years. He had great time for me."

"He had," said John, raking the fire, "Pakie and himself played together for years."

"The fiddle and the concertina," explains Paddy. "Oh God they went lovely together. Pakie could loft it. He wasn't afraid of it."

"He was good," said John, "But 'twas hard to play with him sometimes. He was very particular. If you were a small bit out of tune or blew a wrong note he could get very cranky."

"Pakie liked it right," Paddy says.

Bottle caps pop and another round of porter is served. The six-pack is finished and we're only settling in. Paddy says,

"A good fire is half the battle."

"You can't beat the fire you can see," declares John.

"There's a great tune called 'The Night of the Burnin,'" Paddy recalls.

"I've no names for a lot of the tunes," John sighs.

"We lost them," explains Paddy, "but the main thing is to remember the tune."

"I learned great tunes when I worked over around Kilfenora," John says. "There was a lot of musicians over that way. The best of them was a woman called Mrs. McGrath. She was a concertina player from Ballybreen and she used to make up tunes and all."

"They used to come to her in her sleep," Paddy adds.

"They used, and she used to write the notes on the bedroom wallpaper. She used. Mrs. McGrath played an English concertina and she was the finest player around. A lot of the Kilfenora music came from her. She was great. I have a good few of her tunes. You see, that time musicians only played for dancers, and the music and the tunes were different. Dancers liked some tunes better than others, and not only had you to be a good player but you had to have the right tunes too."

"Some of the new tunes they have now wouldn't do at all," Paddy says.

"So when the dances finished," said John, "the music changed, d'you see? And then you had the radio and the fleadh cheols. Then all these outside players that we never heard of started cropping up, you see, and music from other counties that we never knew about."

"The first fleadhs were great," said Paddy, "I went to a lot of them. One time I went astray comin' home and I ended up in Kilkee. It took me another couple of days to get home. I stopped in Miltown at Martin Talty's for a night on the way."

"We thought he was lost for good," John says.

"A lot of big shots didn't like the music," Paddy says quietly.

"The priests were the worst," John adds. "They used to come and stop the dances. One of them told him (Paddy) he was playing the devil's instrument."

"I told him 'twas my own fiddle," chuckles Paddy.

"He did," agrees John, "you see, there was a lot of drinkin' goin' on at some of the dances—but 'twas harmless enough—and the priests didn't like it. We had a tournament here once and forty-eight teams came to play. The prize was ten pounds. We had a dance goin' down at a neighbor's house and it went on all night."

"'Twas a great night."

"Well a few days after, who comes to the house but the parish priest and he lit me out of it to the high heaven. We were runnin' a house of sin, he said. Hah? Did you ever hear the like of it?"

"Maybe we should play a tune," Paddy says rising from his chair and slipping into a room off the kitchen. He reappears with the fiddle and a canvas bag of clinking bottles.

"I don't know is this beer alright," he says hesitantly, "we have it for a good while."

John rises and comes back with an assortment of whistles and flutes.

Reel with no name: learned from Martin Kiloughry

"The Clarke's whistle was the best whistle ever made," he says. "The key of C. All the old music was played in C."

"I would have to tune down the fiddle."

"There's a lovely soft sound from a fiddle and a whistle in C, but it's not loud enough where you'd have dancers."

"I always play the loud fiddle in pubs."

John blows a timber whistle and Paddy tunes the fiddle. Then they play two jigs they learned from Martin Killoughery, but have no names for them. The clocks tick and Paddy tosses a sod of turf into the fire. John says,

"The Russells were the best ever to remember names of tunes. And they had a lot of stories that went with tunes too. Of course they had Irish, d'you see, and a lot of that history was in Irish."

"Micho has the world traveled with the music. He's a tough man." Paddy says.

"I don't know how he does it with catching trains and aeroplanes and everything. I went to England once and that was enough for me. I went from Liscannor on a coal boat. Myself and a fella called Tom Russell met the Captain below in Walty McHugh's one night and he said he'd bring us to England the next morning for nothing. So we were at the dock at cockcrow with our sandwiches and bottles of milk. Everything was grand and we sailed out into the bay.

The Captain gave us a small little room under the deck and I went to bed, d'you see, I was tired. I don't know how long I slept but I woke up all of a sudden with the boat rockin' and bouncin' and poor Tom Russell on his knees and he prayin'. Hah? I was certain that we were for the bottom. The storm lasted a day and a half and the Captain had to pull into Wales for shelter. Myself and Russell left the boat and got a train to London. That was in 1937.

Isn't it a strange thing, but I couldn't understand London at all and Tom loved it. Work was scarce and I was only getting an odd day here and there. As soon as I had fifteen pounds saved, I came home. I got the Mail Boat to Dun Laoghaire and hired a hackney car to bring me down to Liscannor. The car cost as much as the boat, and I said I'd never leave again."

Then he remembers a reel Martin Killoughery played and Paddy joins in, right foot hopping off the flag floor. They have no name for this tune either, but it doesn't matter.

"The last country dance around here was held in this house," said John.

"The Guards came and stopped it," Paddy said, starting another reel.

"They did," says John and joins him in the tune.

Photo Credits:
P. 104 ©Michael J. Glynne, Courtesy Clare County Library
P. 105 Eugene Lambe
P. 106 Eugene Lambe
P. 107 Eugene Lambe
P. 110 Eugene Lambe

Recordings:

There are no commercial recordings of John and Paddy Killoughery, though they were often recorded by music aficionados. The Irish Traditional Music Archives recorded John and Paddy in 1993 and you can access them at http://tinyurl.com/ldsmsy5

A sample of tunes collected from John and Paddy can be listened to and downloaded from www.eddiestack.com/killoughery.html

Further reading:
'Music from a Timeless Place: John and Paddy Killourhy' by Eugene Lambe. Originally published in Dal gCais, vol.11, 1993.
This article is available online at the Clare County Library website; http://tinyurl.com/n32b5vb

Dancing in Doolin

Up to the end of the nineteenth century, the fashion around Doolin was mostly solo or group step-dancing, to jigs and hornpipes. Micho Russell recalled:

> 'Twas a strange style of dancing, kinda out of time, a jingly classa staggering style. Only the old people could do it...and it died out when I was young. 'Set-dancing' took over from it.

'Set-dancing' originated from 'quadrilles' or 'square dances' brought home apparently by Irish soldiers returning from the Napoleonic Wars in Europe. Dancing masters modified the quadrilles to suit native steps and incorporate traditional jigs and reels. The new format spread rapidly, and each district seemed to adapt the basic quadrille to their own liking. Instead of the solo stepper or single couple, groups of couples took the floor and there was more fun for everyone.

Set dancing bloomed in Doolin. The area had plenty musicians, houses with large flag floor kitchens and a population eager for fun. Wherever there was music, couples stepped from the crowd and flaked out a set—at the crossroads dances, down at the pier on summer Sunday afternoons or at country house dances. The 'set' found a natural home in the cottages, and by the 1920s, country house dancing was the leading form of entertainment and social pastime. Sets were danced at any and every occasion—Weddings, Christenings, Swaries (Wren Boy dances), Strawboy Dances, American Wakes, American Homecomings and eventually Card Tournaments. Micho Russell said:

> At that time I'm thinkin' the type of dances that went on around here were different from any other part of the country. We had every kind of country house dances here, three or four dances every week, Sunday night moreover. An awful lot around Doonagore and that country, and down Ballycotton and over to Moher. A person would come back from America and they'd have a night for them in a house and another one tomorrow night somewhere else. For a finish there might be ten nights for that same person.
>
> What happened mostly was that a couple of musicians would be invited to play and neighbours would be asked over. Two tables would be put together to make a bit of a stage an' musicians used to sit up there on chairs and play. A couple of dozen people or more might show up and they'd be dancin' in the kitchen and they'd be servin' tea and sweet-cake and drink in the parlor or the back room.

If you went to one of these country dances, you'd never ask to leave. My God, but 'twas a lovely time altogether. Dancing sets all night, they didn't know anything about old time waltzes. Late into the night the older people would start singin' and 'twould go on till *maidin geal* (dawn).

THE MOST POPULAR DANCE format around the Doolin area was the North Clare Set, comprising of five figures or segments: the first three were danced to reels, the fourth to a jig and the fifth to a hornpipe or polka. Four couples took the floor for a 'full set' and two couples for a 'half-set'. The half-set was generally performed when space was limited or when two couples wished to give an exhibition. Dancing was taken so seriously that, in some houses, the skull of a horse or a cow had been placed under the stone floor flag in front of the fire, to provide more resonance for battering boots.

The tag of being 'a good dancer' carried respect and was revered and held in as high esteem as musicians. Teachers were often employed to teach children and young adults 'steps' that prepared them for life. Generally these functions were carried out by traveling dancing masters who spent a while in a village and moved on to another. Doolin could support resident masters, as Paddy Pharaic Mhichil Shannon remembered:

> We had great dance teachers here long ago, wonderful teachers. The Slipper Conaola from Inisheer...he was married below in the village. He was called the Slipper because he wore very light shoes and he used to rub the floor with them when he did the steps. Every step was made inches from the floor. There's no dancers like him now, 'tis above in the sky they are when they should be making steps on the floor.
>
> Seanin Droney was another great dancin' master. He lived below in the village for a few years. I remember seeing him dance on top of a porter barrel below outside Connor's pub one day when I was young. He was a small low-sized little man with a black swallowtail coat. A grand gentleman and very respectable. Anyway one day I met him and he said, 'Pat, I hear you have a few steps, you must show them to me.'
>
> So I did, and he said to me, 'Now Pat, don't do it that way anymore, but quickly bring in your left leg and hit the heel on the floor.'
>
> Well, he put a piece into that step and made a great job of it. I'm sorry I didn't learn more from him because he was a great teacher and the last of them around this side of the country.

ARMED WITH YOUR STEPS and a knowledge of the local set, you were off and opportunity abounded. People traveled miles to dances, sometimes taking in more than one on the same night. Listening to the Doolin people talk about these years between the wars, you'd imagine the young and not so young of the area were out all night, every night. The frenzy of dances attests to their position on the totem pole of social activities. Paddy Shannon said:

Great God Almighty, sure for a good few years there was dances nearly every night. Sometimes there might be two or three on in the one night. The worst was thinkin' which one you should go to and thinkin' who might be playin'. They were great and 'tis a pity they ever died out. But in the later years, they could get wild sometimes if there was drink around. And of course after the dances there used to be a lot of roarin' and shoutin' when the young crowd would be goin' home, they had little sense, the craturs. That time too, there used to be a lot of stray asses grazin' the side of the roads and the crowd used catch them and ride them home. Then they'd let the ass into some poor person's garden. 'Twas an awful racket to be at.

Apart from Lent, house dances went on throughout the year. As bicycles became more common, people could travel to a couple of dances in one night. It was non-stop playing for the young Killoughery and Russell brothers, pressed hard between days in the field and nights on the road. As Paddy Killoughery said,

"For a couple of years we didn't go to bed at all. 'Twas all playin'. That's how we got good at it."

STARRY NIGHT IN LUOGH, lighthouse on the Aran Islands blinking across the sea. Batches of people homing in on a country cottage, drawn by the music of flute, concertina and fiddle calling through an open door. Outside for a breath of fresh air and a swig from the bottle of life, groups of men and women are gathered in the farmyard. The crowded kitchen, spectators backed to the walls, in a ring around swirling couples dancing sparks from the flagstone floor. Shouts of "House!", "Around the house and mind the dresser!" Whoops of ecstasy when the battering boots build up into a crescendo. A few musicians sitting on *súgán* chairs, porter bottles beside them, on a makeshift stage. There's no going home till the fun ends. When the musicians down tools, someone sings a song. Then one of the old-timers tells a story that lasts an hour and a half. Dawn arrives and people scatter home as the stars fade into morning. There's talk of a dance in Doonagore the following night.

THE BEST DANCES were when Strawboys came to the house of a newly wed couple, and when Wren Boys held Swaries. The Doolin Wren Boys were one of the most popular groups in North West Clare and had great musicians and dancers. On St. Stephen's Day morn they gathered in Fisherstreet and set off to roam the countryside, playing tunes and dancing sets at every country cottage they called to. The Wren Boys collected a few shillings from the householders. Proceeds of the day went towards a Swarie or Wren Boy's dance, the location of the big night was whispered with a wink and the Boys went on their way.

Held during the twelve days of Christmas, Swaries were the highlight of the season. Dancing in the face of clerical disapproval, Swaries had an illicit atmosphere which added to the excitement. Festive spirit and lots of drink, they lasted from dusk to dawn and were often the first dance a young man or woman attended. Paddy

Shannon remembered:

> A few nights after St. Stephen's day the Wren Boys would have the Swarie in some house or other. It was a great night because everyone was in good form on account of Christmas. Anyone who'd given some money to the Wren Boys on their rounds was invited to the dance, others had to pay some few shillin's at the door. They were great dances and there was drink, tea and whatever else you wanted there for the askin'. The Swaries around here were famous. They went on all night and sometimes they even got a second night out of them. Whatever drink and things then that were left over went to a night just for the Wren Boys themselves…they were called Scrap Parties.

SWARIES BROUGHT huge crowds and sometimes so many arrived that makeshift bars had to be set up in cow sheds. Legends were forged. Late-night mercy dashes were often made to Doolin, Liscannor and Ennistymon for more porter. Eventually, Swarie hosts tired of the huge crowds and the mop-up operation in their wake, and houses became unavailable for the annual Wren Boys' party.

Like Wren Boys, Strawboys were a specific group of musicians and dancers, dressed in disguise, who arrived at your door uninvited. While the Wrenboys had only one outing in the year, Strawboys could have a handful of adventures. Most active in the weeks before Lent, traditionally marriage season in the pre-Vatican II days, Strawboys hit country weddings or when a couple returned from their honeymoon.

STRAWBOYS STRUCK in the darkness of night, disguised in odd clothing, masks, straw robes criss-crossing chests, waists and ankles, headgear of straw, men dressed as women and women as men. Concealing identity was paramount for the Strawboys and their dancers even changed styles so as not to be recognised.

Strawboys gathered in small batches of six to eight dancers and musicians. They came silently to the door, loudly rapped on it, shouted "Strawboys!" They entered the house in a flourish and caused chaotic excitement. Music began and their leader (and best dancer), took the newly-wed bride out on the floor. Other Strawboys picked female dancers from the attendees and a set was performed.

Strawboys had a peculiar code: they refused all offers to drink and eat in the house, but were partial to taking offerings with them for consumption elsewhere. They were believed to bring luck to the newly married couple and there are many theories about their origin. According to some, the custom was a throwback to ancient agricultural fertility rights; others say Strawboys originated as a way for the uninvited to gatecrash weddings and such parties. Another theory says they are reminiscent of a time when reluctant brides were whisked away by their true lovers and his cohorts.

IN THE LULL BETWEEN THE WARS, country house dances were at fever pitch and the clergy got worried. According to the holy men, these social occasions had all the ingredients of Sodom and Gomorrah—couples swinging by the waist without supervision, drink, late nights. Pure pagan stuff.

Sermons were blasted from pulpits and priests raided some country houses, scattering musicians and dancers like Jesus did in the Temple long ago. But Doolin danced on.

As the economic climate worsened, money got scarcer in the West of Ireland. Then some genius got the very bright idea of combining the house dances with a bit of serious card playing and charge a small fee at the door—kill a flock of birds with one stone. All it required was selecting a few houses that were close to each other, put up a turkey, goose, calf or bonham as the prize, get a few musicians and spread the word. On the night, cards would be played in one house and music and dancing in the other. Great entertainment value: a couple of hands of cards and a small hooley to raise the blood. These events were known as 'tournaments' and their popularity spread rapidly. Micho Russell recalled:

> That's when the real big crowds started goin' to the dances. You might have maybe thirty or forty teams of gamblers playin for a goose or something. They'd be four in each team and they paid a shilling or so to enter the game. As well as the card players, they'd be a lot of women there for the dancin', so there were huge crowds. They danced between games of cards. The tournaments were great steam at first but then they classa got out of hand in a few places. 'Twasn't the dancin' at all but the cards, you see. And there might be a fair bit of drink there too and sometimes no goose for the winners and then the racket started rightly. The priests got a bee in their bonnet about them.

The sinful mixture of gambling and dancing to fiddles and concertinas tortured the clergy, who thought this kind of culture better suited to the whiskey towns on the Barbary Coast. Control had to be taken back at all costs and bishops whispered to politicians that morals and money were going down the drain. The peasants were having too much fun, making a packet and causing a racket. Tax them, save them from sin, save them from themselves and their pagan ways.

In 1935, with the prayers of the bishops, the Irish government introduced the Public Dance Halls Act. From now on, it was illegal to charge admission for a dance without having an entertainment license. To hold a dance of any kind, stringent conditions had to be met regarding toilets and health regulations. The Act was confusing and people became wary of organising house dances—threats of law and fear of the wrath of God were enough to warrant a double take on the situation. It took a while for it to take full effect, and then it had a heavy impact on Irish culture.

By the end of the second world war, country house dances were seldom in the Doolin region and there was a big hole in the social calendar. The far-sighted clergy had seen the vacuum coming and built parochial halls to fill the gap. They also selected the entertainment—sober bands playing Irish music and old-time combos that beat out waltzes and foxtrots, safe music for the young and the old.

But while dancers could always cycle or walk to a parochial hall for a bit of entertainment on Sunday night, it was different for the musicians. They lost both audience and venue. Occasionally, Micho Russell and Paddy Killoughery ventured as far as Miltown Malbay to play for dances which went on there regardless of the laws of the land and the church.

The last great dance in the Doolin area was in Killoughery's house. John said:

> About one o' clock in the morn, a Sergeant and a Guard arrived at the door. 'Have you a dance hall license?' the sergeant said. 'No,' says I. 'Well you need a license to hold a dance,' he said, and they came in and counted all the people. The Sergeant told them all to go home and he asked me my name. Well, the following week they were here again with a summons for me. I was brought to court in Ennistymon and fined ten pounds. That was a lot of money in them days, ten pounds. That finished the house dancing all around here, Liscannor, Moher, Doolin. That finished the dancing.

There's still great set-dancers around Doolin and dancing can happen in the bars if the night is right, especially during the Russell Weekend. Flashbacks to when Pakie reigned in O'Connor's and his peers took the floor for a set. Stools were moved to allow more room and onlookers squeezed out of the dancers' way. In a blast of pure spirit, Doolin music and dance entwined, shoes battered the floor and the bar heaved with excitement. Visitors blinked and cameras flashed.

"House, Mary Ann!"

"Around the house and mind the dresser!"

RESOURCES

Breathnach, Breandán: *Dancing in Ireland since 1700*, Dal gCais 5, 1979, pp.39-42

Vaillant, Emery: *Strawboys in West Clare*, Dal gCais 7, 1984, pp. 75-83

Breathnach, Breandán: *The Church and Dancing in Ireland*, Dal gCais 6, 1982, pp. 59-69

Ó hAllmhuráin, Gearóid: *Dancing on the Hobs of Hell: Rural Communities in Clare and the Dance Halls Act of 1935*, New Hibernia Review / Iris Éireannach Nua, Vol. 9, No. 4 2005, pp. 9-18

Doolin Storytellers: Peaitsín Flanagan, Seán MacMathúna and Seán O'Carún, circa 1935

"Tá sé ráite ná fuil sé oiliúnach a bheith ag inseacht scéalta insa lá."
It's said that it's not right to be telling stories during the day.

STIOFÁN UÍ EALOIRE
(1858-1944)

The Storytellers

An Irish speaking area, North Clare was strangely neglected by the Gaelic revival of the late 1890s and early 1900s. Linguistically it was unknown territory and no folklore had been collected there. Gaelic and Irish literary revivalists headed to the Blaskets, the Aran Islands and Connemara but skipped the Clare Gaeltacht. Yeats and Lady Gregory kept their distance, even though their friend Augustus John mentions listening to 'Irish songs and sagas' in O'Connor's in 1910.[1]

As a boy, Micho Russell remembered his father Aughty going up to O'Duilleain's house behind the Doonagore quarries, for nights of storytelling that went on until morning.

> The storytellin' was all in Irish and more than just a form of entertainment. There was stories about Finn and the Fianna and things from history and these are all lost now. More's the pity because they had special meanin's and that's gone too.

In the 1920's, the population of Doolin was just over 800 and falling; Irish was mainly spoken by middle-aged and older people. The younger generation was bilingual but mostly spoke English among themselves.

Unable to find any Irish language folktales from Clare in Dublin universities and libraries, Séamus Delargy, a young founding member of *An Cumann Béaloideas Éireann* (the Folklore of Ireland Society), arrived to Doolin in August 1929. He later wrote:

> I was determined to go to Clare to see what I could find there...the ordinary everyday Irish speech of the commonalty up to 1929 had never been committed to writing, and the oral literature and tradition preserved in Clare in the Irish language had been ignored or its very existence unsuspected.[2]

Delargy traveled from Dublin by train and bus with his luggage and heavy Ediphone recording machine. He hired a car to bring him from Lisdoonvarna to Doolin and the inimitable Peaitsín Mhurty Flanagan got him lodgings with the Carey family in Luogh. Irish was the everyday language of the Carey household; Catherine Carey was from Inisheer and her husband Johnny was a fine speaker of Doolin Irish who happened to be a good storyteller. Delargy spent five weeks with the Carey family and set up his Ediphone recording machine on the kitchen table by the window. There was no electricity so the machine was battery powered. Almost immediately he was recording Irish-speaking tradition-bearers.

> I could not have got better lodgings, for to this house came all the storytellers, singers and musicians, for miles around, and there at various times from 1929 to 1935 I recorded nearly 500 tales and a large body of *seanchas* and extensive vocabularies in Irish.[3]

Delargy found good storytellers and a community eager to help his work. People told him of storytellers in the locality, sometimes bringing them to his lodging. Storytellers were reminded of tales they told years previously, recovering epic sagas which otherwise might have been lost for all time. He made the acquaintance of many of the local tradition bearers and recorded from Peaitsín Flanagan, Johnny Carey, Michael O'Tiarnaigh, Aguistin O'Duilleain, Padraig O'Duil, Tomas Maoldhomhnaigh and Sean MacMathúna. The reception Delargy received in Doolin moved him. He was the first stranger to experience the storytelling tradition there, and was euphoric by the collection of folklore and folktales he brought back to Dublin in September 1929.

SÉAMUS DELARGY

THE FIRST PIECE of Doolin folklore to be published appeared in *Béaloideas* No 2, (1929 -1930). It had been collected from Johnny Carey by Delargy, who later wrote in *The Gaelic Storyteller*:

One of the finest Irish speakers I met there was a certain Seán O'Carún (Johnny Carey) of about seventy years, a man of keen perception who readily understood the object of my visit. Some months later I learned from his wife that when he was not to be found, he had gone into a cave in the mountain above his house, to wrestle with his memory, striving to recall tales which he had heard from a native of the Aran Islands, some forty years before, and which he had forgotten: he returned in triumph with three of these tales restored to their home in his memory, and I wrote them down.[4]

DELARGY RETURNED to Doolin for Christmas that year and lodged again with the Carey family. He set about collecting as soon as he settled and recorded from Sean O'Danachair, Donnacha O'Maoldhomhnaigh, Padraig MacMathúna, Daithi O'Conchuir, Sean MacDeid, Sean O'Caoili, Aughtie Russell, Michael Flannagáin as well as those he met on his previous visit. His presence brought storytellers out of the shadows and all were anxious and intent in having their stories preserved. Several of the longer stories he heard were learned from a cooper named Tomás O Conaola, an Inisheer man who came to Doolin to make barrels for salting fish and lived in Luogh fifty years before.

On December 22nd, Delargy met and recorded Paddy Sherlock, a travelling chimney sweep from nearby Ennistymon, who told Delargy a selection of stories in English. The Sherlock family had a reputation for being good storytellers and Patrick's grandfather had years previously told these same stories in Irish around Doolin.[5]

IT WAS DURING this second visit, and almost by chance, that Delargy first met Stiofán Uí Ealaoire, a gifted storyteller in the traditional mode, but about whom nobody had said a word. Delargy gives a vivid account of the occasion at Moloney's house near Fisherstreet bridge on January 3rd, 1930.

Anthony Moloney had arranged for us to gather in order to give me an opportunity of getting acquainted with some of the old people whom he specially selected as being likely informants and of service to my work. I paid for a bucket of porter fetched from a local pub, there was a good fire blazing in the hearth, the sky was covered with frosty stars, and the faint murmur of the sea seeped in through the door.

A memorable night of storytelling followed, each old man giving it his best. Anthony kept order, but the people themselves were so interested that they listened with great attention and in complete silence to the songs and stories, which lasted for five hours. This was the first time I met Stiofán Uí Ealaoire, who proved to be the best Irish speaker and storyteller I was to meet in Clare, and he was the lion of the evening.[6]

Stiofán was 72 years old, a bachelor, and lived alone in a tiny thatched cottage in Ballycullane. He was poor and lived frugally, keeping a few hens, a cat and a cow. A well-liked, humorous man, he was a fluent Irish speaker and fond of good company and late nights beside the fire. None of his friends however knew that he was a storyteller of the old tradition until that night he made his debut in front of Delargy's Ediphone machine. The two men became close friends and over the following years Delargy collected over 150 tales from Stiofán, as well as *seanchas* and Irish vocabulary.

ANTHONY MOLONEY'S COTTAGE

DOOLIN MAN Paddy O'Connor told Séamus O'Dea about a recording session in Carey's shortly after Delargy had 'discovered' Stiofán

> The evening that Stiofán was the principal performer saw him seated in the center of a circle of other performers in front of a big fire in Carey's kitchen. On the extreme left of the circle was Seán Carey and beside him Simon Flaherty (Inisheer), a brother of Seán's wife. Near the front of the fire was Seán McMahon (MacMathúna) and Darby Griffey, while near the center sat Johnnie Devitt and Aughty Russell, who were expected to contribute some songs. And right in the centre sat Stiofán with Séamus Delargy on his right with his notebook and pen. The remaining places to the right of the fire were taken by Jack John McMahon, Dick Moloney, Frainc William McMahon, Peaitsín Flanagan and Mike Donnochu (Styke?).[8]

After Stiofán had told a story or two and he and the audience were warmed up, Delargy set up the Ediphone. Mrs. Carey served tea and scones and when everyone was refreshed and the cups and plates cleared away, the recording began.

Over the years, in this same kitchen with his Ediphone machine on the table by the window, Séamus Delargy collected nearly 500 tales and a large body of folklore. This is one of the finest repertoires of folktales from any area in Europe, but only the tail-end of what must have been a vast treasure of stories, *seanachas*, proverbs, verses and old words which had slipped into oblivion with the decline of the Irish language and social change. It's unthinkable what might have been the fate of Doolin's folktales and storytellers if Delargy had not come to Clare to be, as he said himself, 'an eleventh-hour chronicler.'

DELARGY WAS also the catalyst that drew together people who had an interest in storytelling. His recording machine and the transformation of Stiofán from a nice poor illiterate soul to high-level tradition-bearer lent a curiosity to the collector. He describes a snowy night in January 1930 when Johnny Carey and himself came to accompany Stiofán to Carey's house:

> The night was full of stars and the wind was keen in our faces as we walked the snowy road which brought us home. Johnny Moloney, a friend of Stiofán's, came with us. When we arrived we found Peaitsín Ó Flannagáin and some others. Tonight was a really exciting one—story following story—and I was kept busy with my notebook and the Ediphone.

IN DOOLIN, Delargy collected several different types of stories: tales from the Fiannaíocht, hero and voyage tales; tales of magic, tales about historical figures and even a love tale or two. Some of these stories came from the Aran Island and Brandon in West Kerry. Most of the Aran stories were learned from Tomás 'The Cooper' Ó Conaola, who was a fine storyteller with a good stock of stories.

Storytelling is a communal art that's as old as the hills. Storytellers were born into a tradition of tale telling, and they listened to, assimilated and remembered stories like the lyrics of a song. Tales were chosen to suit the teller's talent as well as listeners' reaction to them. And no two storytellers would tell the same hero-tale in precisely the same fashion. Years could pass between a tradition-bearer first hearing a story and telling it at a gathering—or as in the case of Stiofán Uí Ealaoire, several decades. Storytellers had an extraordinary memory for detail and gave full scope to their imagination, sometimes interspersing their own observations on life and impressing their own personality on a story. A good command of the Irish language was essential to carry the story and tellers often enhanced them with inflections of the voice, gestures and mood, so they became alive and seemed more credible. They weaved their creativity and the traditional stories together to provide a performance. Delargy said that Stiofán's command of Irish and his artistry in storytelling was "one of the oldest one-man shows on earth." At sessions, certain things were expected, as Delargy noted:

> Above all, it was required of the narrator to include at certain times in the narrative, passages of high-flown and obscure rhetoric, which were so appreciated by the audience.

Seán Ó'Carún (Johnny Carey) 1929

The folktales opened up a fantastic world where little distinction was drawn between the natural and the supernatural. Through the stories, moral and cultural values of the community were unconsciously conveyed and as they stretch back into the past, some give a glimpse of old beliefs and supply information on local history and lifestyles not so readily found elsewhere. Delargy likened the world of the storyteller to 'another Hidden Ireland', a place so rich in folklore that it had few equals, yet its international importance was more appreciated abroad than at home. He believed that the Irish oral tradition had a vast amount of hitherto unnoticed information on the social life of the ordinary country people, and was a vast new resource for historians:

> The only real authorities on Irish tradition are the storytellers; they belong to a different world from the commentators. And even the best-equipped collector, must cultivate academic humility and a feeling of respect and reference with the exponents of ancient lore.[9]

In Doolin, there were very high standard relating to the long hero folktales. The three components of storytelling were plentiful in the area: a stock of great stories, gifted tellers, interested and attentive audiences. Many in the audience might know the story themselves, and storytellers reacted to their presence, their interest and comments of approval. There would be active storytellers at the gathering who expected more than a bit of entertainment and they could be merciless in their criticism if justice was not done to the story.

At the end of his notebook on this Clare visit, Delargy wrote of a story being told:

> This is the worst told tale I have ever heard, and to one familiar with it, the omissions, hesitations and inconsistencies were exasperating. The audience was quite disgusted. Now and then I would catch the eye of Johnny Carey, and Stiofán Ó hEalaoire, who were sitting beside the fire smoking, and they would shake their heads sadly. To them it was a sacrilege to mishandle a story. Finally, old Carey could not stand the strain no longer, being outraged beyond endurance, and he shouted at the storyteller, telling him what he had omitted and admonishing him.[9]

ONE OF THE REGULAR visitors to Carey's house was Seán MacMathúna, a shy man who didn't at first contribute to Delargy's collecting. He was a good listener, a middle-aged man who had very pure Irish. Delargy got to know him and discovered he could read and write in Irish and came

STIOFÁN UÍ EALAOIRE AGUS SEÁN Ó'CARÚN

from an old literary family. One of his ancestors was the poet and teacher Donnacha an Chairn who had a school near Ennis, at the end of the 18th century. He had a great love for the Irish language and culture and was deeply saddened that it was slipping away. Realising that Seán could help in collecting folklore, Delargy appointed him to continue his work in North Clare.

Delargy returned to Doolin on August 2, 1930 and set up his base in Carey's house. On August 15, Stiofán came to him and told a version of a well-known folktale called '*Conall Gulban*'. The long episodic tale took over two hours to narrate and Delargy had never heard anything so good. A magnificent story that showed Stiofán as a first rate-artist, it was recorded on the Ediphone at Carey's on August 26, before an audience of seventeen people. Twenty years later Delargy would say it was "the finest tale I have ever heard before or since."

IN 1930, The Royal Irish Academy (*Acadamh Ríoga na hÉireann*) began recording the various Irish language dialects around the country, under the direction of Dr. Wilhelm Doegan. On September 18, Delargy hired a car in Lisdoonvarna and headed for University College Galway with Johnny Carey, Stiofán, Liam O'Duilleáin and Séamus Ó'Cillstrutháin. They recorded in a little room off the University Archway with Professors Liam

Ó'Buachalla and Tomás Ó'Máille. Stiofán told two stories: *Billy Teabhras* and *Fear a bhí Ruite Bocht*. These recordings give an idea of Doolin Irish and Doolin storytelling.[10]

ON AUGUST 29TH, 1932, Delargy made his third expedition to Doolin and collected more tales and folklore from Stiofán. He was in Stiofán's cottage on September 11 and wrote:

> In the house with Stiofán and myself are: Peaitsín Ó' Flannagáin, Johnny Carey, Séamus Maloney of Doonagore and an ex-soldier, Johnny Maloney, who comes nearly every night to visit Stiofán. The old man has been talking of the fights he took part in the old days of the cattle driving. Stiofán is one of the finest Irish speakers I have ever known. It will never be possible to bring back the language the way he speaks it. And how little attention is now paid to these fine old Irish speakers by the stupid talkers of today.[11]

On this trip Delargy spent three days in Kilbaha in South-West Clare and returned to Dublin on September 19th.

Seán MacMathúna walked the roads of North Clare on Sundays and holy days in search of oral tradition. He thought little of going twenty miles for a story or a piece of *seanchas*. In one instance he made several visits and covered 118 miles to collect information from an informant. When he had a notebook filled with material he sent it to Delargy in Dublin, where his handwritten material was cataloged and typed.

Seán also attended events where tradition-bearers were likely to gather, such as fairs, markets, sports, games and feiseanna. In the mid-30s he was at a feis near Miltown-Malbay with Paddy Killoughery and Micho Russell,[12] when they met Martin Talty, Willie Clancy and Bobby Casey for the first time. MacMathúna went to an all night-music session with them and walked back to Doolin at dawn.

IT WAS NOVEMBER 1937 before Séamus Delargy got back to Doolin. Every piece of material he had recorded between 1929 and 1932 was written in notebooks that he brought with him. Stiofán had lost his sight at this stage and was living with a relative, Padraic Ó'Dábhoireann of Doonagore.

Every day, from morning to night, Delargy checked his manuscripts with their informants. It was a slow job and each day Johnny Carey and himself visited Stiofán, who was his most reliable source. He was saddened by his old friend's blindness and his absence from the nights at Carey's house.

> The scenes familiar to me in 1929-1932 are repeated: the old friends gather at Carey's to chat, tell tales, sing songs I have heard so often but like to hear again. Peaitsín Ó' Flannagáin is here, now 75 and looking much older than formerly. Johnny Carey now 80 but still full of energy—unchanged as they all are really. Seán MacMathúna, a mere lad of 60, is there too. The children of John Carey Junior gaze open-mouthed at

the 'Irishman' as I am known locally, who has come from the big city of Dublin to collect old stories.

I am privileged in knowing these Clare people, these last Irish speakers of Corca Morua (Baroney of Corcomroe, the Burren). In a few years they will be gone and the old world will have gone with them.[13]

After a week in Doolin, Delargy believed he had finally achieved the goal he set in 1929: he had collected what folktales existed in Doolin. In the process he had recorded at least twenty storytellers and Clare Irish as spoken by the ordinary people, the last batch of native speakers. He had collected what *seanchas*, folklore and vocabulary as he could and his diligent friend Seán MacMathúna was digging out nuggets of oral tradition in his wake. The folklorist returned to Dublin and noted:

Made the run in record time with a carload of records and transcripts. Well pleased with my trip, with the worry long on my mind about the Clare collection at long last dispelled and done with.[14]

DELARGY CAME BACK to Doolin in January 1943 and spent time with Johnny Carey, Peaitsín Ó Flannagáin, Seán MacMathúna and Stiofán. There were storytelling sessions like the old days, but the participants were fewer and Stiofán was confined to home.

When Delargy called to say goodbye to Stiofán, there were tears in their eyes as if each knew it was for the last time. Stiofán clasped Delargy's hands and said in Irish, "If you're here the night that I'm waked, I'll tell you a story." Stiofán died the following year on the fourth of May and was buried the following day. Seán MacMathúna wrote to Delargy with the news. Stiofán was 86 years old. A week later Delargy received another letter from Doolin, dictated by Peaitsín Ó Flannagáin and written in Irish by a neighbour. It was one of the few letters Peaitsín had ever 'written' and began: "I am sorry to be telling you that our soft, sweet, Irish storyteller Stiofán is buried, may God have mercy on his poor soul."

Delargy later wrote:

Stiofán was the best Irish speaker that I met anywhere in Ireland. It is a great loss to modern Irish scholarship that no Irish linguistic expert ever made a study of his marvelous expressions and his equally rich vocabulary. He had hundreds upon hundreds of words and turns of phrase that were not found anywhere else in Munster. I was the first stranger to appreciate his stories, and to listen enthralled to his inexhaustible flow of untrammeled Irish, which up to then no pen had recorded. When his name is mentioned in *Tuath Clae* by the bay, they'll talk about his craft, about his magnificence as a storyteller, about the funny habits he had, about the turns of phrase that he had. I collected from Stiofán, with the help of the Ediphone, enough (tales) to make a lovely big book if the collection is put into print sometime.[15]

The stories were later published as *Leabhar Stiofáin Uí hEalaoire*, a monument to the storytelling tradition of Doolin.

SEÁN MACMATHÚNA continued to collect stories and folklore in North Clare and he kept pressing further afield. He met Séamus Ennis when the music collector visited the area in September 1945, but thereafter they had little contact with each other. For twenty years Seán walked the roads and boreens, searching out Irish speakers and oral traditions. When he died in 1949, he had written over 11,000 pages of all kinds of folklore and his experiences as a collector in North West Clare.

IN 1951, DELARGY returned to Doolin with producer David Thompson of the BBC World Service. They recorded Paddy Sherlock telling The *Black Dog of the Wild Forest*, *Manus*, *The Golden Bird of Phoenix in the Land of Youth*, and *The Beauty of the World*. Delargy had collected these from Paddy back in December 1929 and had also recorded the original Irish versions of the four stories from Stiofán, Seán O Carún and Seamus O'Diolún.

Paddy's inimitable style enthralled listeners when his stories were first broadcast in July 1951. The programme was repeated several times over the next couple of years.

Of the hundreds of stories told in Irish around Doolin, only a dozen or so crossed the language frontier from Irish to English. They did however hold the same verve and vitality in the telling as their old Irish counterparts. Through the BBC, Doolin storytelling tradition found its largest audience even as it was on its last legs.

Delargy visited Doolin over the following years, often with an academic colleague interested in folklore. He called on old friends that were still alive and said a prayer at Killilagh graveyard for those who had passed on. Johnny Carey was the last of the storytellers, and when he was bedridden in 1955 at the age of 95, Delargy visited him. It was an emotional parting, both men failing to hold back the tears. Johnny took his hand and in the old manner kissed it.

> I had said goodbye to the man from whom I had written the first folktales in Irish in North Clare, and I had said goodbye to the old world of which I had been privileged to be an eleventh-hour chronicler.[16]

FEW OF THE YOUNG PEOPLE were interested in learning the ancient art of storytelling. Times had changed and their grasp of the Irish language was too limited to allow them to enjoy or learn the stories. For the most part, the old stories died with their tellers and by the late-fifties the vast majority of those Séamus Delargy had collected from had passed away.

Séamus Delargy retired from directorship of the Irish Folklore Commission in 1973 and set about bringing the Clare collection into print. By then the old *Tuath Clae* storytellers were all buried and only a handful of native speakers were alive. The organizing of the material and editing was a daunting job and he received help from a young folklore scholar, Dathaí Ó hÓgáin. He intended the first volume of the collection to be devoted to stories and traditions he recorded from Stiofán and worked toward that goal. Séamus died on June 25, 1980, knowing his wish would be fulfilled. The thought he expressed in Béaloideas No 14 (1944) of "a lovely big book if the collection is put into print sometime" would become a reality the following year with *Leabhar Stiofáin Uí Ealaoire*. Collected and edited by Séamus Delargy and prepared for publication by Dathaí Ó hÓgáin, the book was published by *Comhairle Bhéaloideas Éireann* in Dublin. It is a fitting memory to both storyteller and collector.

Delargy's interest in storytelling revived the practice somewhat around Doolin and Stiofán began to tell his stories in the cottages. Paddy Shannon remembers him coming down to Fisherstreet during the winter nights and gathering with a few Irish speakers.

He often came down to Annie Rosie's house below in the village. She was a great *Irisheen* like most of the old people. I remember him well, sitting below beside the fire, he wore small round spectacles and the cap was down on his forehead. He had great stories—all in Irish of course and he could put so much into a story that you'd swear you were there.

Micho Russell could remember parts of stories Stiofán told and had passages of the fight scenes from *Madra Dubh na nOcht gCos*, which were aired at certain times during the story like the chorus of a song.

THE ART of the storytelling tradition remained and was evident in the telling of yarns, biographical epics and shorter bits of folklore which were reborn in English. Most of these traits were unconscious and are the last remnants of an oral tradition: the Russells had them as did Paddy Shannon and other Doolin tradition-bearers. Pakie Russell was probably king of them. He could weave strings of Irish and English together and stitch a patchwork of bits of old folktales—with maybe passages from the Bible. Through some alchemy it all became a story.

THE FOLLOWING TWO STORIES were collected by Séamus Delargy in Doolin. I have translated them from the original Irish and tried my best to retain their vitality and atmosphere. Ever aware that these stories were meant to be listened to rather than read, the written word cannot truly do them justice, especially across the language frontier,

The first story was told to Delargy by Seán O'Carún during Christmas 1929. A humorous anecdote about a piper, it was one of the first pieces of Clare oral tradition to be published and appeared in *Béaloideas* No 2, (1929-1930).

"Hie Over to England!" was told to Delargy by Stiofán Uí Ealaoire and is a magic tale about a journey with *na daoine maithe*, or the fairies. In the 'spell,' *Each a's gath dhó-sa*, means 'a steed and a spear for him'. The story is included in *Leabhar Stiofáin Uí Ealaoire*.

Seán Ó Carún (Johnny Carey)

Scéilín gan Anim (Story without name)

There was a piper here long ago and he was gone from home for twenty years. He was coming home this night and he had enough drank. He was passing the graveyard and he said to himself,

"Many good man has been buried here since I left. I have to play a tune for them!"

He went into the graveyard, sat down on a tombstone and began to play music.

Another man was passing by and he had enough drank. When he heard the fine music he said,

"By gor, I'll go down and dance a stave!"

He went to the closest tombstone to the piper and began to dance. The piper didn't stop or the dancer didn't stop 'til he had enough danced.

"If your living is alive," said the dancer, "you're Eamonn!"

"I certainly am, Seán!" said the piper.

That was when they recognised each other. Which of them was the bravest?

Stiofán Uí Ealaoire

"Hie Over to England!"

A man lived here in the hills, a place they call The Green Hill, close to us here, and it's not a long time ago at all. Seán Long was his name. He had a small, lovely house, sheltered and tidy, and his wife kept it very clean. The 'good people' (fairies, spirits) used to visit there now and again, to eat and drink as they went their way.

One night of nights, they were getting ready to go over to England, to rob a strong drink store that was in London. They hit down the road to Seán's house and ate food. They were eating their fill, and if they were, Seán woke up. Beyond in his bed he listened to the visitors all over the house. He bent and looked over at them; he was gentle and quiet. He knew well who was there.

That was grand. He was looking at them and when they had the food eaten and were going out, every one of them dipped their finger in a cup at the head of the table and said:

"*Each agus gath dhó-sa,*

Agus Hie over to England!"

He rubbed on his forehead whatever stuff was in the cup. That was grand.

Seán was beyond, he was looking at them all, and they going out after they did that. He jumped out of the bed beyond, wearing nothing but a night-shirt. He came to the cup, stuck in his finger and said:

"*Each a's gath dhó-sa,,*

Agus Hie over to England!"

Out through the roof of the house went Seán, like everyone else. He didn't stop going after them until they reached London City. They went into the store they were going to rob and Seán went with them. That was grand. They were all doing their own business inside and Seán was looking at them coming and going. But, of course, the poor man liked a drop of drink. He tasted some drink, and when he tasted it, he tasted it again and again. But he drank too much of it. He got drunk and went to sleep beside a barrel.

In the morning, when the workmen came into the store to work again, they discovered it had been robbed. They looked every single place and could not find how the robbers entered the store. They were going through the store when they came on Seán and he thrown at the bottom of a barrel, in a deep, drunken sleep. They picked him up. They didn't know what to make of him. They took him with them and put the law on him and put him in prison until the day of the court.

When the court day came, Seán was in his shirt and stood on a bench before the judge. And the judge didn't know what to make of him. When the judge asked him a question, Seán didn't know how to answer and he didn't know what was being said. Anyway if he answered, the judge wouldn't know what he was saying, at any rate.

Whatever in the world kind of glance Seán gave, he saw a little man coming through the roof of the building. The little man stood behind the judge and made a sign to Seán.

He said:

"*Each a's gath dhó-sa,*

Agus Hie over to Ireland!"

Seán settled himself and said

"*Each a's gath dhó-sa,*"

"Hie over to Ireland!"

Out went Seán through the roof of the building. What people were in the courthouse fainted and thought it was the Big Man who was there.

That was how Seán escaped. It was early afternoon at home. And when he was going into the meadow in his nightshirt—his family came to him. He didn't know on the face of the earth how he spent the previous day and night.

Stiofán Uí Ealaoire's cottage, Ballycullane, circa 1935

Leabhar Stiofáin Uí Ealaoire
(Stephen Hillary's Book)

Just over fifty years after Séamus Delargy recorded the first folktale from Stiofán Uí Ealaoire, a book of his oral traditions was published. Máire MacNéill says it should have pride of place in every Clare library. It certainly deserves it. *Leabhar Stiofáin Uí Ealaoire* is a very special work, an insight into 'the hidden Clare' through beautifully told folktales. Even though the printed word cannot trump the storyteller's voice, Stiofán's spirit comes through in these pieces, his gentle personality and mastery of the art of storytelling. If the psyche of county Clare ever needs a liturgy, I sincerely hope *Leabhar Stiofáin* is part of it.

Before the book appeared, I had known a little about Stiofán from Paddy Pharaic Mhichil, Pakie and Micho Russell. A few short snatches from his stories were known and aired when his name came up. Micho would mimic his way of way of telling a story. We heard rumors that Stiofán's book was due and waited. But I don't think anyone had any idea of what a powerful book it would be.

I don't remember the publication date, just heard or read that it was available. I tried Kenny's of Galway, but it was sold out. A friend tried a few shops in Dublin, but what few copies they had were gone. There was a bit of bafflement, a book in Irish by an unknown Clare storyteller was in demand. Who would have thought? The next time I got to Kenny's, the last copy had just been sold. Mrs. Kenny took down my name and promised to keep a copy for me.

On November 4, 1982, I was strolling down Shop Street in Galway, when my friend Paddy Williams from Kilshanny pulled up on his racing bike and said,

"Kenny's are after getting in Stiofán's book. Go down now."

And I did. I won't forget that day.

As an aspiring writer back then, I was smitten by *Leabhar Stiofáin Uí Ealaoire*. By the stories, by the art of the telling and crafting. By their sense of place. In their timelessness, magic realism, grit realism and pace, I saw parallels with the Latin American writers like Fuentes, Marquez and Mario Vargas Llosa.

THERE ARE over three hundred pages of tales in *Leabhar Stiofáin*. That's the size of a novel, a lot of story to keep in the head. Séamus Delargy says this was only the tip of the iceberg, a small portion of the repertoire that the storyteller once had. Every story he could remember he gave to Delargy and Seán MacMathúna but not all of them are in this book. Stiofán could not read or write, but he was far from being illiterate with his storehouse of oral literature and traditions.

At the beginning of the book, Stiofán talks about storytelling:

> I heard the old people telling the stories and I growing up as a young boy. I had a great interest in listening to them and I liked the stories and I fell into the habit of learning them myself. When I'd be working in the garden myself, I used to be remembering the old stories and telling them to myself in my mind, so that I'd keep them in my mind. I liked listening to the old people, I was a follower of the old people who told the stories.
>
> When the long nights used to be there, neighbors would gather to listen to the old men who told stories. They spent the night until late in the night listening to them. As long as they were talking and telling stories, every person had to be silent. They didn't mind because every one of them was happy to be listening to the talk.

When Stiofán was a young lad, stories from the *Fiannaíocht* about Finn and the Fianna were popular. His father Michael was a good teller of *Fiannaíocht* stories, but died when Stiofán was only 3 years old. His neighbours Briartach Ó Flannagáin and Dáthaí MacMathúna were good Fenian storytellers. His mother told Stiofán that several nights Dáthaí and Briartach came to the house at nightfall and began telling stories with his father. By the break of day they would have each only told one story.

Leabhar Stiofáin includes Hero Tales; Tales of Magic; Romantic Tales; Stories of Thieves and Tricksters; Humorous Tales and Anecdotes; Religious Tales; Legends of the Dead; Fairy Legends; Mysterious Phenomena; Magic; Poets and Poetry; Strong Men and Heroic Deeds; Drowning and Rescue; Daily Life; Varia—a potpourri of little bits and pieces including prayers.

APART FROM Dathaí MacMathúna, Briartach Ó Flannagáin, Seán O' Maoldomhnaigh and his own mother Cáit, Stiofán attributed stories he knew to fourteen local storytellers. When young Stiofán was growing up, there may have been as many storytellers as musicians in Doolin.

Leabhar Stiofáin is difficult to find in bookshops but can be bought online from *Comhairle Bhéaloideas Éireann*, http://tinyurl.com/nnnszvs. If you've enough Irish to understand it, buy it. It's a gem. And apart from the stories, it's a beautiful record of Doolin Irish.

References

1. John, Augustus, *Chicaroscuro*. Johnathan Cape, 1952. pp. 70

2. Delargy, Séamus, *Oral Tradition of Thomond*, Eugene O'Curry lecture, University College Dublin, November 29, 1962

3. *ibid*

4. Delargy, Séamus, *The Gaelic Story-teller*, Cumberlege, London, 1945

5. *Béaloideas*, Comhairle Bhéaloideas Éireann, Dublin, XXX, 1962

6. *Leabhar Stiofáin Uí Ealaoire*, Comhairle Bhéaloideas Éireann, Dublin, 1981. pp. xviii

7. Delargy, Séamus, *Foras Uí Chomhraí Lecture*; Kilkee, County Clare, May 10, 1968

8. O'Dea, Séamus, *A Premiere for Stiofáin*; Dal gCais No.6, 1982

9. Delargy, Séamus, *Oral Tradition of Thomond*, Eugene O'Curry lecture, University College Dublin, November 29, 1962

10. *Doegan Project*, audio of stories by Stiofáin and other local storytellers at http://tinyurl.com/lana5bu

11. *Leabhar Stiofáin Uí Ealaoire*, Comhairle Bhéaloideas Éireann, Dublin, 1981. pp. xxii

12. Stack, Eddie, *Doolin*, Micho Russell, p. 75

13. *Leabhar Stiofáin Uí Ealaoire*, Comhairle Bhéaloideas Éireann, Dublin, 1981. pp. xxi-xxii

14. *ibid*

15. *Béaloideas*, Comhairle Bhéaloideas Éireann, Dublin, XIV, 1944

16. Delargy, Séamus: *Oral Tradition of Thomond*, Eugene O'Curry lecture, University College Dublin, November 29, 1962

Resources

Leabhar Stiofáin Uí Ealaoire: Comhairle Bhéaloideas Éireann, Dublin, 1981

Seamus Delargy and North Clare: Máire MacNeill; Dal gCais, No.6 1982.

Paddy Sherlock's Stories: Dal gCais, No.6 1982.

A Premiere for Stiofán: Séamus O'Dea, Dal gCais, No.6 1982.

Folklore Collecting in Co. Clare: Tadhg O'Morchú's Third Visit (1950): Patricia Lysaght, *Béaloideas*, No 76, 2008, pp. 139-192

Photo Credits

P. 119 ©National Folklore Collection, UCD

P. 120 ©National Folklore Collection, UCD

P. 122 ©National Folklore Collection, UCD

P. 123 ©National Folklore Collection, UCD

P. 125 ©National Folklore Collection, UCD

P. 126 ©National Folklore Collection, UCD

P. 133 ©National Folklore Collection, UCD

The Gentry

At the opposite end of the social order from the tradition-bearers and the plain people were their gentry landlords. Boetius MacClancy and Francis MacNamara were Doolin gentry who created chaos in their lifetimes, Boetius in the 16th century and Francis in the 20th. In a way, they bookend Clare history: Boetius welcomed the English and Francis said goodbye to them. Both were learned men and fluent in several languages. Boetius is remembered as a cruel tyrant and Doolin black sheep. Francis was well-liked and best remembered for bringing artists and writers to Doolin in the 1910s. He started out as a poet and finished life as a hotel owner, breaking a lot of rules and hearts on the way.

The MacClancys

Boetius MacClancy came from an ancient Clare family and their earliest *Tuath Clae* settlement was in Cahermacclancy. Noted for their learning, they later had a small castle in Toomullin and as hereditary Brehon Lawyers to the O'Briens of Thomond, they held the most fertile land around Doolin rent-free. They were an integral part of the Irish law system in Thomond and all legal documents and agreements required their inspection and signature.

In medieval times the MacClancys had a school of Law and Poetics near the site of the present Catholic Church at Knockfinn. It was renowned throughout Ireland and a great many students came to study there. The school flourished for centuries and the MacClancys prospered. They were known as noble, hospitable people, patrons of the arts and connoisseurs of fine wine.[1]

Boetius Óg MacClancy, Professor of Brehon Law and Poetry, died in 1576 and his nephew Boetius became head of the family. Highly educated and fluent in Latin, Irish and English, Boetius was the Clare legal brain at a pivotal period in history. The Crown was making inroads and the gentry were jittery. Boetius was privy to their fears and political leanings. His neighbours the O'Connors, who held Doonmacfelim Castle and Doonagore Castle, became increasingly worried about the encroaching English forces. Boetius drew up the deed that granted O'Connor land to Turlough O'Brien of Ennistymon, in lieu of his protection. He witnessed the deed on Jan 2nd, 1582 at Doonagore Castle, which came into his possession within a few years.

MacClancy would have been consulted by the county chieftains prior to the indenture that changed the ancient district of Thomond into an English county, a major step in dismantling the traditional Irish system of law and land ownership. It is thought Boeius was bribed by Sir John Perrott, Queen Elizabeth's Lord Deputy in Ireland to lobby the county chieftains to accept the indenture. Below is an abstract from the document, which places Thomond (Clare) in Connaught.

Indenture, dated the 17th of August, 1585, between Sir John Perrott, knight, of the one part, and the Lords spiritual and temporal, chieftains, gentlemen, etc. Of that Part of the province of Connaught called Thomond. "Witnesseth, that all Irish titles shall be abolished; the inhabitants are to grant to the Queen ten shillings a year for every quarter of land containing one hundred and twenty acres that bears either horn or corn, in lieu of all other demands, save the raising of horse and foot for her Majesty..."[2]

MacClancy allied himself with the new order, changed religion and pledged allegiance to the Red Queen. Unlike the vast majority of Clare gentry, he was allowed to hold his land rent-free. Later in 1585, when Parliament was convoked in Dublin, Boetius was one of the representatives sent from the newly constituted county of Clare.

Thither went Turlough, son of Teige, son of Conor O'Brien; and also Lord of the Western Part of Clann-Coilein, namely MacNamara; and Boetius MacClancy, the second Knight of Parliament to represent the county of Clare.[3]

Hereditary Brehons and scholars of the time had a high social position in Irish life. Some of these intelligentsia families became specialists in land transactions under the new British system and were well capable of manipulating the laws. Boetius added considerably to the family largess, often by underhand-means. He was a landlord, but unlike his ancestors, he had little time for the common people, evicting those who couldn't make rent and terrorizing those that could.

MacClancy became High Sheriff of Clare in 1588 and was not long in office when ships from the Spanish Armada were storm-swept down along the west coast of Ireland. The Lord Deputy's orders were to 'execute all Spaniards and seize all treasures, hulls of ships, stores, munitions. Torture is acceptable if necessary.' On September 16th, Boetius was informed that two ships were near the Aran Islands.[4] Another anchored off Liscannor and a small boat went ashore and got provisions from the locals. One unfortunate Spaniard got arrested and his ship, the *Zuniga*, left Liscannor without him. It eventually found safe haven in La Havre in France.

The other ships were not as lucky. Both the *San Esteban* and the *San Marcos* went aground on September 20th. *San Esteban* sank at the White Strand near Doonbeg, as MacClancy's agent Nicholas Cahane reported,

"God hath cast to shore a great ship from San Sebastian wherein were 300 men all drowned but three score or there about."

A few miles north, the galleon *San Marcos* was wrecked on a reef near Mutton Island with a massive loss of life. A third ship may have been wrecked near Ballaghaline.[5] Upwards of 700 Spaniards perished in the worst maritime disaster off the Clare coast.

Boetius took the Lord Deputy at his word and plundered the ships. He arrested 170 survivors and took them to Doonagore Castle, where they were sentenced to death. With the assistance of Sir Turlough O'Brien (in whose district the *San Marcos* went aground), a Captain Mordaunt, Messrs. Cusack and Morton, Boetius executed the Spaniards at *Cnoc an Chrochaire,* (Hangman's Hill) near St. Catherine's. The unfortunate men were buried in a mass grave without distinction of rank, name or birth. MacClancy's brutality was commended by the English and praised for his zeal and loyalty. The Armada set the tone for his tenure as High Sheriff.

It was believed that Boetius took a huge hoard of Spanish treasure from the shipwrecks. Beautiful silver and gold ornaments and jewellery were reported to be in his various houses, along with old chests and casks of wine. He presented a massive table from one of the ships as a wedding present to his brother-in-law, Conor O'Brien of Lemanagh. The ornately carved oak table ended up in Dromoland Castle with four cannons from the Armada.[6]

SPANISH ARMADA TABLE AT DROMOLAND CASTLE

While still in good stead with the English, MacClancy had Knockfinn constituted a Manor and had his rent-free status extended. In 1590, he was appointed arbitrator in a bitter dispute between the Earl of Thomond and the descendants of Malachy O'Loughlin of the Burren. The agreement seems to favour the Earl more than the O'Loughlins, his neighbours. The deed was drawn up by Gilbert Davoren, from Cahermacnaughton law school, hereditary Brehons to the O'Loughlins. It was signed on June 9th, 1590 at Knockfinn and witnessed by Boetius who signed his name in Irish.[7]

After peace was made with England, consent was given to one high-ranking Spanish nobleman to exhume the body of his son (who was executed by Boetius), and bring it home to Spain for burial. The Spaniard's remains couldn't be identified from all the skeletons in the mass grave and this caused diplomatic discomfort. The English are said to have reprimanded Boetius for taking upon himself the power of life and death against enemies taken in war.[8]

Boetius died in 1598 and was survived by his son Murtach MacClancy. Fifty year later, the MacClancys of Knockfinn lost every acre and house they possessed to the Cromwellian settlers. The MacNamaras would later own the entire MacClancy estate.

Séamus Delargy and Seán MacMathúna both collected folktales about Boetius around Doolin and one is included in *Leabhar Stiofáin Uí Ealaoire*. Most of the tales concern the ill-gotten treasures MacClancy is supposed to have buried before he died. Clues to the location of the treasure are given in dreams, sometimes by Boetius himself. But the treasure is never found.

Boetius was appearing in people's dreams three hundred years after his death, so deeply set was he in the folk memory and psyche of the people. Going on clues from a dream, Paddy Pharaic Mhichil Shannon went hunting for Boetius' treasure as a young man.[9]

REFERENCES

1. Frost, James, *The History and Topography of the County of Clare* CLASP, Clare Library online. http://tinyurl.com/ldeo35u

2. Ibid

3. O'Donovan, John (editor): *Annals of the Four Masters, Vol 6*. Hodges & Smith, 1851. pp. 2050

4. *The Spanish Armada*, CLASP, Clare Library online. http://tinyurl.com/mbpt5a8

5. Spellissy, Seán, *The Armada in Clare—The Doolin Connection*, The Clare Association Yearbook, 1988, pp. 18-21

6. Westropp, Thomas J, *Relics of the Spanish Armada in Clare and Sligo*. The Journal of the Royal Society of Antiquaries of Ireland, Ser. 5, Vol X, 1900. pp. 92-95

7. Dwyer, Philip, *The Dioceses of Killaloe from Reformation to Close of the 18th Century*. Hodges and Figgis, Dublin, 1878. pp .230

8. Spellissy, Seán, *The Armada in Clare—The Doolin Connection*, The Clare Association Yearbook, 1988, pp. 18-21

9. Stack, Eddie, *Doolin*, The Way We Were, p. 59

The MacNamaras

Well connected to the O'Briens, the MacNamaras were a premier old Clare family who lost most of their estates and wealth in the Cromwellian campaigns. Teige MacNamara of the Cratloe and Knapogue clan moved to Ballyvaughan in North Clare in 1659. He had seven sons, but only the sixth survived until manhood. Bartholomew MacNamara began his family's ascent by marrying Dorothy Brock, daughter of the Mayor of Galway. Her dowry was a house on twenty acres near Galway city. The couple moved to Gleninagh Castle a few miles on the Doolin side of Ballyvaughan where their son William was born in 1714.

By a series of strategic marriages, the MacNamaras leapfrogged from Gleninagh to Doolin and onwards to Ennistymon. Every move increased their property, land and wealth. On the way, they converted to Protestantism—more a political move than a religious one. Colourful, eccentric and hard players, they were well-respected by the native Irish and grasped the ropes of the English system. They became High Sheriffs of Clare, represented the county in Parliament and held top positions in the English army and Royal Navy. Their marriages were often marred by family infighting, betrayal and plain misfortune.

William MacNamara brought the name to Doolin from Gleninagh in 1748 when he married Catherine Sarsfield, co-heiress with her father of 1,400 acres of land and several large houses. Their marriage was darkened by a long drawn-out family squabble with Catherine's six brothers. Each had served 'illegally' with the Irish Brigade in France, and by English law they had lost their inheritance rights. Ultimately the law won, and so did the MacNamaras.

William's heir, Francis, had another difficult marriage. In 1774 he wed Jane Stamer of Cornelly House, Clarecastle and built Doolin House soon afterwards. Jane was a well-connected but tortured soul who grew estranged from her children. After Francis died in 1821, she tried to alter his will and their eldest son, William Nugent, took her to court. He won and inherited most of his father's estate. His siblings got Aran View at Knockfinn, St. Catherine's at Gortaclob, and houses in Oughtdara and Moher.

William Nugent was a widower and father of six children. His wife, Susannah Finucane of Ennistymon House, had died young in 1816. Known as The Major, William never remarried and lived in Doolin House. Well-liked by both poor and gentry, he served Clare with distinction for seventeen years as Liberal M.P. In 1843, Ennistymon House and the O'Brien estate came to him after his brother-in-law, Andrew Finucane, died without an heir. The Major passed away in 1856, owning vast amounts of land in North Clare. His only son Francis inherited the estate.

Unlike his ancestors, Francis had a long bachelorhood and enjoyed his time between Doolin House and Ennistymon House, a noble dwelling overlooking the Inagh river. According to Ennistymon folklore he had a fondness for young women and liked to call for them in the middle of the night. His nickname was 'The Terror.'

Francis designed the streetscape of Ennistymon, much of which still stands. At age 58, he married Helen McDermott, daughter of a Dublin solicitor. A few years later, they moved to an upgraded and extended Ennistymon House. His eldest son, Henry Valentine was 12 when Colonel Francis died in 1873.

Henry Valentine was educated at Harrow in England and later at Cambridge. More English than the native English, he was known as H.V. and called 'The Reverend' behind his back. In 1883 he married Englishwoman Edith Elizabeth Cooper and their first child Francis was born the following year. The family resided at Ennistymon House, spending summers in Doolin.

Victorian, severe and a die-hard Unionist, H.V.'s most endearing quality was an occasional flash of MacNamara humour. One of the biggest landowners in the county, he received annual rents in excess of £10,000 from 700 tenants, and had property in Galway, Dublin and London. Unfortunately he lacked his ancestors' finely tuned antennae for gauging political moods and shifts.

By birthright, his son Francis was set to inherit a huge estate and considerable wealth. Francis had an idyllic childhood roaming the woods around Ennistymon, fishing and boating on the river. Summers were spent at Doolin House and as a child he entered local folklore by sailing down the Aille river in a bathtub. He could have been swept out to sea if a woman called Mary Rosie hadn't rescued him at Fisherstreet bridge. The youngster was known as Master Francis to the locals, a name that stuck with him to the end.

Like H.V., Francis went to Harrow to be educated. He was happy there, becoming friends with Lady Gregory's son Robert. Francis showed academic promise, so H.V. gave him an allowance of £250 a year to study law at Oxford. Robert Gregory was also there, passing time before going to study art at the Slade School under Welsh painter Augustus John.

Francis dropped out and by 1904 was calling himself a poet and living in London. Robert Gregory was about, having inherited a house in Chelsea from his father. Gregory introduced Francis to Augustus John. Doors opened easily for MacNamara; tall, lanky, blue-eyed and good-looking, he had charisma and nobility and was regarded

BOOKPLATE FROM H.V.'S LIBRARY

in the salons of Chelsea as a poet, philosopher and free-thinker. Yeats thought him the finest speaker in the land.[1]

In July 1907, Francis married Mary Majolier in London. Half-Irish and half-French, she preferred to be called Yvonne. Her parents disapproved, as did H.V. who severed his son's allowance. The couple honeymooned in Ireland, staying with Robert Gregory at Mount Vernon, in New Quay, Clare and at Coole near Gort with Lady Gregory and Yeats.

On the birth of his grandson John the following year, H.V. renewed Francis' allowance. 1908 was a year of shocks for H.V. Tenants were restless with his half-hearted land reforms, but he seemed unconcerned until the Doolin Cattle Drives happened. Stiofán Uí Ealaoire took part in the first one when over fifty men cleared livestock from MacNamara land on September 12th 1908:

> Stock belonging to Colonel Tottenham and Messrs. T. McCarthy, James Linnane and Coleman O'Loughlin were driven off grazing lands about Doolin, held by them on the eleven-month system from Mr. H.V. MacNamara.[2]

Eight policemen unsuccessfully tried to stop another cattle drive on Sept 20th. Forty-three Doolin men were charged and tried in Ennistymon on September 30th. It was a tense day with 400 policemen drafted into town and thousands of farmers packing the streets in support of the Doolin Drivers. The seriousness of the case drew the presence of the police

The Doolin Cattle Drive

In the last days of September
When our boys were sent to jail,
They marched them to the station house
And sent them off by rail.
The Bobbies who escorted them
Were itching for a row,
For nothing irritated them
But the How! How! How!

The Peelers started chargin'
And the boys were flinging stones,
Harrison got frightened
And shouted out to Holmes:
"I think we're much mistaken
In kicking up this row,
For they'll drive us like the bullocks
With their How! How! How!"

Long life to you O'Brien,
You're locked in a prison cell;
To your loyal comrades
History will tell.
With courage bold they did their work
And manfully were seen
That day in Ennistymon
When we unfurled the flag of green.

Micho Russell's version of 'The Doolin Cattle Drive'.
There are a few of songs about the event.

County Inspector, D.I. Richard Cruise, who was married to H.V.'s daughter, Doreen Finola.

Court proceedings were interrupted by chants of 'How! How! How!' from the supporters outside and the racket of cudgels beating the ground. D.I. Cruise ordered Inspector Harrison to quell the crowd with a baton charge. It was unexpected and brutal. Several supporters and innocent bystanders were injured and shops where people sheltered were wrecked.

Forty drivers were sentenced to fourteen days in Limerick prison. To bring them to jail, the police baton-charged the crowd again to clear the street. Though they eventually managed to take the Doolin men away, the police were overpowered when the crowd fought back. The bloodshed on the streets of Ennistymon marked a turning point in the history of North Clare and a more astute MacNamara would have heeded the warning signs. Stiofán Uí Ealaoire called it *Lá an Bhaton Charge*. He said that that day broke H.V.'s heart and he never had a good day after that.[3]

Because of these troubles, Doolin House and its adjacent buildings became temporary barracks for a squad of constables and two officers. When the drivers were released in October, police went on high alert. The men arrived on the West Clare Railway and were greeted at Ennistymon station by the town brass band and thousands of supporters. The Doolin contingent carried cudgels and led a wide march from the station through the streets. The police withdrew to barracks and to Ennistymon House. There was no disorder, just joyful music and song, punctuated with shouts of 'How! How! How!' The tide had turned.

H.V. BEGAN TO IMPLEMENT land reforms and the situation quietened. The police left Doolin House and Francis spent the following summer there with Yvonne and baby John. He was happy in Doolin, swimming at the beach and walking along the shore. Fisherstreet was mostly Irish speaking and Francis began to learn the old language. Local people heartily welcomed him and he became good friends with their 'king', Cuckoo O'Brien. Paddy Pharaic Mhichil Shannon said:

Master Francis he was called, he was over six-foot two and as fine a man that ever crossed the bridge into Fisherstreet. The people here had great time for him, he was like one of our own. All he ever cared for was boats and fishin' and talkin'.[4]

DOOLIN CATTLE DRIVERS, 1908

In London Francis and Yvonne lived on their families' allowances, while he wrote poetry and yachted on the Thames. In 1909 Francis published 'Marionettes', his only book of poetry. It contained a number of poems about the Ennistymon river and one for his son John.

Francis' family grew, and in annual succession Nicolette, Brigit and Caitlin arrived. Their summers were spent in Doolin House, which had an open welcome to artists and bohemians. The Bloomsbury and Chelsea sets visited, as did the Irish crowd. Francis introduced his visitors to the local culture, often bringing them to O'Connor's (then Shannon's). They were captivated by the music, songs and stories—throwbacks from another era. Francis, Cuckoo and Augustus were known as the 'Unholy Trinity' and their escapades were remembered around Doolin until the 1980s. Paddy Pharaic Mhichil said:

> They used to cause awful rack where ever they went. They used to wake the people here in the village at all hours of the night, and they comin' back from the sea and they singin' like larks, wherever they had been.

On a living-room wall of Doolin House, John painted a fresco of a group of country women in shawls against a local landscape. He also painted the young Fisherstreet beauties and illustrated old Irish legends in pen and wash as he listened to Francis tell them. Augustus became a champion of Francis' work, telling a friend:[5]

A poem from Marionettes

Diminutivus Ululans
(To John MacNamara)

Wailing diminutive of me, be still
Or cry, but spare me that regretful tone,
Of sorrows elemental waxing shrill,
O you of living things the most alone!
Son, do you thus reproach me and make moan,
Because upon Love's chariot I did fly
And a horn winded in the great unknown,
Calling your atoms out to be an I?
Should I have let you in abeyance lie,
Disintegrate another million years?
Then use your life to teach you how to die
And pass again beyond the reach of tears,
Some day you may regret I dragged you thence,
Perhaps forgive the vast impertinence.

Marionettes can be downloaded free from
http://tinyurl.com/pp2npcu

He has shown me a manuscript which to me seems most remarkable. He has put soliloquies into the mouths of personages from the Irish legends, and he has made them talk quite modern language albeit in free verse—the result is amazingly vivid and vital. The people live again!

Wild and unfettered in Doolin, Francis' shouts of "Down with the bourgeoisie and all their lying conventions!" were in tune with the revolutionary cries of his father's tenants—"Land for the people, the road for the bullock." John noted the police were wary of him, but the locals treated him with a deference which sometimes embarrassed him.[6]

Francis on Doolin Beach circa 1910

H.V. juggled political time bombs while Francis wrote poetry, philosophized on Doolin Beach and ploughed the seas with Cuckoo. Doolin House was one big commune, added to every so often by the arrival of some writer, artist, philosopher or misguided genius.[7]

In parallel with the rebellious Irish mood of the time, Francis impressed on his visitors that all rules, regulations and conventions were taboo in Doolin. Free love and open relationships were encouraged. Some couples could take this in their stride, while others fled. There were wild parties and nudity on the beach, hair-raising voyages across to Aran with Cuckoo and pub crawls in Galway.

But despite Francis' many unconventional friends holidaying at Doolin House, it was his fraternising with the tenants that really galled H.V. He got a lukewarm welcome at Ennistymon House when he visited with his wife and children.

Francis came to Doolin in the summer of 1914 while Yvonne and the children stayed in Hammersmith, preferring the comforts of London to Clare. He wrote, pleading with her to join him, but she declined. By then he was thinking that their marriage was a mistake.

The following summer he returned alone again to Doolin and with the war, it was a quieter sojourn. In a letter[8] to Augustus John he wrote:

"I was never so glad to get away…into the open fields; the grey stones of the Burren were like a purge to my spirit."

Sons of the gentry felt it their duty to join the fight in WWI. Francis' only brother George was already in the British Army, but he hesitated. His friend Robert Gregory signed up in September, 1915, and later Augustus enlisted. Francis dithered. MacNamara political intuition may have told him to stay out of it; it wasn't his fight. He was also aware of the mood and state of Ireland and supported Sinn Féin. This was an embarrassing blow to his Unionist father

1917 was a bad summer for H.V. In May, his son George was killed in France and a while later, de Valera topped the poll for Sinn Féin in the East Clare by-election. Ennistymon celebrated the victory by flying tricolours from houses; bonfires were lit on the streets and the local brass band paraded around the town.

About this time, Francis fell for the beautiful but fickle Euphemia, wife of painter Henry Lamb and left his family. H.V. was furious and banished him from Ennistymon House. Although the affair lasted only a few months, Francis and Yvonne never reconciled. They remained good friends, though he failed dismally to support her and the children. They went to live with Augustus John's family at Alderney Manor in Dorset after the break-up.

1918 began with news that Major Robert Gregory had been mysteriously killed during a training exercise in Italy. His plane was seen flying at 2,000 feet, then went into a spin and crashed.[9] Francis was numb, Gregory was one of his oldest friends and a fellow bohemian. He would have known about Robert's dream years earlier of dying in a plane crash. This is immortalised by Yeats' "An Irish Airman Foresees His Death."

Cuckoo O'Brien

On February 27, 1918, County Clare was declared a full-blown military area.[10] Carrying a gun was forbidden and passports were issued to people leaving and entering the county. *The Clare Champion* newspaper was suppressed and mail and telegrams were subject to censorship. Extra troops were brought in to support police. North Clare had an active IRA battalion, brazen enough to march through Ennistymon in 1919. That December, H.V. and a hunting party were ambushed in the Burren. H.V. was shot in the arm and after the incident Ennistymon House was under armed guard night and day. At a later compensation hearing, when asked how the injuries impacted him, MacNamara replied that he found 'lifting a decanter of claret difficult.'

The Black and Tans came to Ireland in 1920 and The War of Independence went into full tilt. H.V.'s income was shrinking; tenants were refusing to pay rents and funds from those who had purchased lands weren't forthcoming. Police and British military billeted at Doolin House and Francis stayed in England, scraping by on the kindness of friends. Some of the time he spent in London with the Chelsea and

Bloomsbury crowd; other times he appeared unexpectedly in New Forest and stayed for a while with Yvonne and the children. Then he took off wandering again. He would have been stopped in his tracks by the news from Clare following the events of September 22nd, 1920.

The Rineen Ambush near Miltown Malbay and its aftermath rattled H.V. A turning point in the War of Independence, it was carried out by IRA volunteers from the Mid-Clare Battalion. They ambushed a police patrol, killing its five members and one Black and Tan. The IRA took their weapons and ammunitions and burned their vehicle. Suddenly a convoy of British soldiers on another mission appeared and the IRA took them on. The gun battle lasted three hours and several soldiers were injured. The IRA got away, carrying their two wounded men to safety.

The British were outraged and reprisals were brutal and immediate. Local farmers were arrested, hay and houses burned, and people were shot. That night a mixed force of police, British soldiers and Black and Tans burned several houses in Lahinch and killed a number of people suspected of being connected to the rebels. One volunteer was burned to death in his girlfriend's attic and her invalid sister also died in the fire.[11] The Crown mob continued to Miltown Malbay and burned eight houses there. The police rampaged through Ennistymon, smashing shops and torching them. They killed a number of people including Tom Connole, a local trade union secretary, whose brother Joe was a friend of Francis.

It may have finally dawned on H.V. that this crisis was not going to pass over like the other ones. Security around Ennistymon House was boosted with two gun-toting sentries at the gates and constant patrols and snipers. H.V.'s excursions from home became less frequent, and he was always accompanied by an escort and a detail of soldiers.

A truce between the rebels and the Crown went into force at noon on July 11, 1921. The peace was fragile but held until a Treaty was signed in December.

The end came quickly for H.V. and weeks later, Doolin House was razed by Black and Tans withdrawing from Clare. This was seen as retaliation against Francis' Sinn Féin sympathies. A letter from the Mid-

Mid-Clare IRA Battalion at Liscannor Training Camp, 1921

Clare IRA dealt H.V. the final blow in April 1922. He was ordered to vacate Ennistymon House and informed that all his property was confiscated by the IRA. He fled to London and never returned. Ennistymon House became barracks for the newly formed Gardaí.

Francis came back to Clare in the summer of 1922 to assess the damage to Doolin House. It was a roofless black shell with the wind blowing through the empty windows. The sight upset him and after a spell with old friends in Fisherstreet, he returned to London. He was back the following year, intending to convert the stables into a studio and living quarters. After a few weeks he ran out of money and gave up on the idea.

FOR A WHILE FRANCIS lived on a houseboat on the Thames, subsisting on onions and dried peas, trying to write poetry and formulating Marxist theories about life and economics. He edited the *Wessex Review*, a short-lived magazine and translated prose and poetry from French to English for small publishers. His wife and children moved to a permanent home on the edge of New Forest but he seemed aimless. Remembered then by friends as a penniless poet in tattered clothes, he was helped by a lover of means for a time. This ended when he had an affair with Lillian Johnstone, an Aran woman working in London. She had a daughter, Patricia, which Francis acknowledged as his.

H.V. died in 1925 as a result of a fairground accident at Wembley Stadium in London. Francis benefited from his will, though much of the property was frozen by the new Irish state. He set out to claim his inheritance and spent more time in Ireland, also seeing a role for himself in shaping the fledgling nation.

He came to Coole Park on January 6th, 1926 and Lady Gregory was happy to see him. He stayed for Richard Gregory's 17th birthday party. Richard was Robert's son and some of the local gentry gathered to celebrate the occasion.

Lady Gregory noted that he "helped to keep things lively." She wrote in her diary:[12]

Francis MacNamara talked of his economic plans for Ireland, very interesting. He will talk them out with Keynes before publishing. He has been studying the movements in other countries toward this end, and has had Soviet papers translated for him. The Russian experiments extremely interesting, but he says drawn up as if by very intelligent schoolboys. And the misery and waste caused by Russian experiments are terrible.

FRANCIS WAS LUCKY that he had friends in court—Yeats and Gogarty were Senators—and others who remembered his allegiance with Sinn Féin in the early days of the revolution supported his claim. He eventually received a fraction of H.V.'s estate. He did regain Ennistymon House and the surrounding lands, as well as the ground-rent rights to the town. Most of the Doolin estate had percolated back to the tenant farmers. Finally a man of means, in 1928 he formally divorced Yvonne and married Augustus John's sister-in-law, Edie McNeill.

Edie stayed at their London flat while Francis enlivened Ireland. He had a house in Dublin and mixed with writers and thinkers of the new nation. His attempts at poetry seem to have petered out as he expounded more and more on economics and financial theories. Nicolette, his eldest daughter, came to visit him in the summer of 1928, accompanied by an Irish school-friend, Iris O'Callaghan, whose family he knew. Francis charmed Iris, laying the foundation for a future love affair. He brought the girls to Coole Park on August 23 and, as ever Lady Gregory was delighted to see him.[13]

> Today Francis MacNamara came to call, with his daughter and a Miss O'Callaghan; so happily Yeats was here, he and Francis had a good talk chiefly I think gossip over the John family. John likes the priest son best, who keeps him in order when there.

Francis took Nicolette to Ennistymon and explained his plans to convert the ancestral home into a hotel. He brought her to Doolin and they went sailing to Aran and Connemara on his Galway hooker *Mary Anne*. Some days they made a connection, other days they were miles apart. Nicolette wanted to study art at Slade and Francis gladly paid her fees and gave her an annual allowance.

A FEW YEARS EARLIER he had met Pamela L. Travers, an Australian writer enchanted by Irish poetry, myths and folklore. Invited to Dublin by A.E. Russell, she frequented the literary salons. Travers worshipped Yeats but fell in love with Francis, seeing him as a 'great Irish poet and critic, a great friend…very beautiful, fair, highly intellectual.'[14] By the early 1930s, they were having an affair.

Francis and Edie had a flat in London's Regent's Square and unannounced, his youngest daughter Caitlin moved in with them. Caitlin was determined to be a dancer, though not making much headway. Francis and herself had constant rows, each trying to outwit, outshout the other. They were similar in character, and Caitlin could rip him apart with well-aimed barbs. Then he'd sulk and disappear and spend time with Pamela Travers, who was also in London.

Travers was very much in love with Francis and thought he would divorce Edie and marry her. She sent him her first Mary Poppins manuscript in 1932. No lover of children's literature, he was reluctant to read it. The work impressed him and he wrote back:[15]

1930 BOHEMIANS IN WALES: FRANCIS MACNAMARA CENTER BACK ROW, TOWERING OVER AUGUSTUS JOHN

Why didn't you tell me? Mary Poppins with her cool, green core of sex, has me enthralled for ever.

Travers felt that Francis understood Mary Poppins better than she did. The book was published in 1934 and became a best-seller. Francis and Pamela partied until he got restless and left to attend to his other life.[16]

Though Caitlin moved out, his world got more complicated. Iris O'Callaghan was on the fringe, living on the *Mary Anne* which was docked on the Thames. Sometimes she visited Regent's Square, which unnerved Edie. Later she moved into the flat and slept on the couch in the study. When Francis announced that Iris was his Muse, Edie moved to the country. She died shortly afterwards and Travers expected Francis to propose to her, unaware that he had another interest.

FRANCIS AND IRIS had just moved to Dublin when daughters Caitlin and Bridget arrived from London. The girls occupied the basement and Caitlin made it clear that she despised Iris, who was just three years older than her. It was upstairs-downstairs: his daughters lived frugally below while Francis and Iris entertained and dined extravagantly above. To make amends, he brought Caitlin around the Dublin literary and theatrical hangouts; she met Liam O'Flaherty, Seán O' Casey, Michael MacLiammór and Hilton Edwards. They went to Yeats' salon and Caitlin took a dislike to the poet, whom she regarded as pompous.

THE FALLS HOTEL

MAYBE IT WAS TO KEEP the peace in Dublin that Francis sent Caitlin west to Ennistymon with a lorryload of furniture. Plans for the hotel were progressing and loans were secured. Independent from him, Caitlin embraced Ireland and remembered this period as one of the happiest and care-free times of her life. She hadn't been in Clare since she was a toddler, yet it was warm and familiar. Family friends welcomed her home as if they'd known her all their lives; she was Francis' daughter and they said she was 'a real MacNamara'.

Caitlin lived in the best rooms of Ennistymon House. She swam in the river, walked the woods and glens and danced on the lawns. Some nights she went to country house dances in Doolin, where Cuckoo and his family looked after her like she was one of their own. Cuckoo's daughter Kitty became a close friend.[17]

When Francis came to begin renovations, Caitlin's lifestyle was cramped. He complained that she was spending too much time carousing, sometimes not coming home at night; she accused him of being hypocritical. When Iris arrived, the gulf between father and daughter widened, but she wouldn't budge from Clare —it was her ancestral ground too and she belonged there.

ENNISTYMON HOUSE was renamed The Falls Hotel and Francis painted the new moniker in huge white letters on the roof facing the town. On the front lawn he erected the figurehead from an old sailing ship—a blonde, bare-breasted woman looking at the cascades. Inside, murals of the mythical sunken village of *Killstuipheen* and a *poitín* distilling scene decorated two walls. He stocked the cellar with fine wines, hired staff and opened for business in early 1936.

Caitlin worked as barmaid and waitress, but was constantly at loggerheads with Francis and Iris. Finally she left for England and Augustus John introduced her to Dylan Thomas shortly afterwards. Francis thought Dylan a 'mediocre poet' and had little contact with the couple. Poetry wasn't treating him well. He fell out with Yeats for not including him in the *Oxford Book of Modern Verse* in 1936. He was stung by W.B.'s dismissive remark to mutual friends:

> Francis MacNamara had some poetic talent once, but he lost it by not attending to the technique of verse.

DYLAN THOMAS AND CAITLIN, 1937

IN 1937 FRANCIS told Pamela Travers that he was marrying Iris and she fell apart. Her biographer wrote:[18]

> The loss of MacNamara represented a serious passing of hope for Pamela, and left a great emptiness in her spirit. Pamela cared for him a great deal more than he ever knew. She carried a torch for Francis MacNamara for the rest of her life, forgiving him, preserving him in her mind as the perfect man, though she knew all along he was a Don Juan.

Iris was manageress/hostess of the Falls and rarely without a glass in her hand. The food was good: all local fare, with emphasis on fish—salmon and sea trout from the Ennistymon river, Doolin mackerel and lobster supplied by Cuckoo. Guests were mainly friends of Francis and came from England and Ireland. Local doctors, teachers and politicians frequented the bar, which seldom closed. Sometimes there was no charge for drink, room or table, because Francis believed good company was better than money.

The writer Kate O'Brien spent a summer there and wrote about Francis and the hotel in her book 'My Ireland.' She relates a meeting between de Valera and Francis who recommended that Dev "Establish a House of Princes. Restore its rightful prince for each county." Francis offered himself as prince of Clare. Dev was mute and afterwards told his aides, "Please don't ever let that man near me again."

The Falls brought life and style to Ennistymon. Francis was lord of the manor and played the part: he had a batman-cum-chauffeur; an old horse-drawn carriage was renovated and he occasionally travelled with a bugler on the back to trumpet his approach. But the hotel was losing money and to keep it afloat he sold most of the best pasture land on the estate. There were other problems—Iris' drinking was out of control and Francis' health was failing. With the outbreak of World War II, business nose-dived and the hotel only opened sporadically.

During the war, Francis and Iris spent most of the time in Dublin and their relationship crumbled. He was attending doctors regularly but the cause of his illness was unclear. His deterioration terrified Iris and her drinking increased. Francis left her and moved to a small flat on Baggot Street.

PAMELA TRAVERS was now very wealthy and they got in touch in 1940.[19] She wanted to adopt a child, preferably an Irish child with good genes. Francis arranged a solution—the daughter of a poet friend (Joseph Hone) had given birth to twin boys who were being offered for adoption.

Before Travers left London for the babies, she consulted an astrologist who advised her to only take one of them. Hone was upset by her decision

IRIS, 1935

but despite his arguments, Pamela returned to London with one baby. The business would later become a disaster for her and both twin boys.

IN MAY 1941, The MacNamaras were stunned when John was arrested in Portsmouth on suspicion of murder. He was a Royal Navy Lieutenant on the *HMS Hood*, a battle-cruiser which was pride of the British fleet. On shore leave in Portsmouth, John was in a dockside bar when a brawl erupted and a man was killed. He was among several drinkers who were arrested and locked up. *HMS Hood* left port without him and headed to the Denmark Strait to intercept the German battleship *Bismarck*. On May 24, *Hood* was hit by several shells and exploded. 1,415 men perished without a trace and only three survived. In the meantime John MacNamara was released uncharged by the police in Portsmouth.[20]

FRANCIS LEASED The Falls and came there in 1944 to spend the summer in the guest lodge. He visited Cuckoo in Doolin and they had a few good days before his health failed and he was rushed to hospital in Dublin. On his discharge he was cared for by daughter Pat and when Nicolette visited him, she was taken aback by the shell that her father had become. The sheriff was after him; bank loans were delinquent and he had nothing to show for his life. He knew he was dying and said where he wanted to be buried. Yvonne visited him and returned to England deeply saddened. Low on luck, he had few friends and Bridget and Nicolette came back to Dublin to help care for him.

Francis summoned Danny his batman from Ennistymon[21] and ordered him to burn all his bank statements, check stubs, manuscripts, letters and papers. That may have been the fate of Francis' unpublished work—an extensive autobiography, thoughts, theories, plays and poems on which he sporadically worked throughout of his life.

AMIDST MEMORABILIA from his early days and a Doolin painting by Augustus John, Francis MacNamara died on March 8, 1945, in a room overlooking the sea in Dalkey. The poet who introduced Bohemia to Doolin had sailed away to the otherworld. In his *Irish Times* obituary Joseph Hone wrote:

> I am not alone in feeling that his pretensions to some superior understanding and integrity of intellect had some basis in reality. He broke a good deal of crockery on his way through life—that of others as well as his own—but I have never heard that he made an enemy. Perhaps only Ireland could have produced a Francis MacNamara: and only Ireland could have failed to give direction to his remarkable gifts.

FRANCIS, EARLY 1945

Forty years later in Doolin, Paddy Pharaic Mhichil Shannon remembered:

> Master Francis was last of the gentry around here and he was the best of them. My father taught him Irish and 'tis many the night he sat here by the fire when we were little children.
>
> Before the last big war, he started up the Falls Hotel and that was his downfall. I heard that there was no rhyme nor reason for what went on there. Poor Francis was kind of careless and lost everything for a finish. But even when he was losing it, he thought of the people in Doolin. Every Christmas a big chest arrived from Dublin or wherever he was and it would have a pig's head, tea, cocoa, sugar, treacle and things like that. They were called 'Christmas Boxes' and always created excitement. A good few of the families used to get boxes from Francis. He remembered the Doolin people right to the end.

Francis MacNamara, 1884-1945

Photo Credits

P. 145 Seán O'Connor, Fisherstreet

P. 147 ©Nicolette Devas Estate

P. 148 unknown

P. 149 Courtesy Clare County Library Photo Collection

P. 151 unknown

P. 152 Courtesy Clare County Library Photo Collection

P. 153 ©Nicolette Devas Estate

P. 155 ©Nicolette Devas Estate

Portraits

P. 154 Iris O'Callaghan by Anthony Devas. Painted at Regent's Square, London, 1935.

P. 156 Francis MacNamara by Gerald L. Brockhurst. Etching on creme paper, London, 1920. Acquired by The National Gallery of Ireland in 2009.

References

1. FitzGibbon, Constantine, *The Life of Dylan Thomas*, J.M. Dent & Sons, 1966. pp. 118

2. National Archives of Ireland: CO/904 166

3. *Leabhar Stiofáin Uí Ealaoire*, Comhairle Bhéaloideas Éireann, Dublin, 1981, pp. 5-6

4. Conversation with Paddy Pharaic Mhichil Shannon

5. Augustus John letter to Quinn, Irish-American lawyer and literary supporter, August 6, 1912

6. John, Augustus, *Chicaroscuro*, Johnathan Cape, 1952, pp. 70

7. Devas, Nicolette; *Two Flamboyant Fathers*, Morrow, 1967. Francis' daughter gives a good account of summers at Doolin House before WWI, pp. 25-33

8. Ferris, Paul, *Caitlin, The life of Caitlin Thomas*. London, Pimlico, 1993. pp. 16

9. *History Ireland*, http://tinyurl.com/or9rsqy

10. Coogan, Tim Pat, *The Man Who Made Ireland — The life and Death of Michael Collins*. Robert Reinhart, 1992. pp. 85

11. Conversation with Seán Ó Súilleabháin, Quin, Co Clare

12. Lady Gregory's Journals, vol 2, Book 1

13. Lady Gregory's Journals, vol 2, Book 31

14. Lawson, Valerie, *Mary Poppins She Wrote: life of Pamela L. Travers*. Simon & Schuster, 2013. pp. 167

15. Ibid.

16. The film *Saving Mr. Banks* gives some insight into Pamela's character. Her biographer, Valerie Lawson suggests that Travers wrote 'Mary Poppins' for Francis.

17 Ferris, Paul, *Caitlin, The life of Caitlin Thomas.* London, Pimlico, 1993. pp. 48

18. Lawson, Valerie, *Mary Poppins She Wrote: life of Pamela L. Travers.* Simon & Schuster, 2013. pp. 185

19. Lawson, Valerie, *Mary Poppins She Wrote: life of Pamela L. Travers,* Simon & Schuster, 2013. pp. 187

20. Conversation with Nicholas Monton, great-grandson of Francis MacNamara in Doolin, August 2014. George Tremlett, Caitlin's biographer, told him the story.

21. Conversation with Jimmy Stack, Ennistymon.

Resources

Two Flamboyant Fathers, Nicolette Devas, Morrow, 1967

Caitlin—the life of Caitlin Thomas. Ferris, Paul, 1993

Caitlin—life with Dylan Thomas, Caitlin Thomas with George Tremlett

The History and the Topography of the County Clare, James Frost. CLASP, Clare Library online

Augustus John, Michael Holroyd, Vintage, 1977

The MacNamaras, Colm Shannon, Doolin, unpublished thesis, GMIT, Galway

Mary Poppins She Wrote: life of Pamela L. Travers, Lawson, Valerie, Simon & Schuster, 2013

Ennistymon House and Falls Hotel, Clare County Library article, http://tinyurl.com/5m5prosb

Some Tower Houses of North Clare, Risteárd Ua Cróinín and Martin Breen; The Other Clare, Vol 16 1992, p 5-10

The MacNamaras of Doolin & Ennistymon, Michael MacMahon; Dal gCais, No 11 1993

Index

A

American Wakes 29, 112
An Fear Bréige 10
Aran Islands 9, 10, 35, 50, 60, 62, 100
Arensberg, Conrad M. 29, 51, 89
Aughavoher House 13, 27

B

ballad boom 93
Ballaghaline 13, 19, 27, 30, 38, 62, 139
Ballinalacken 10
Banríon an Bháire 78
Bárr Trá 74, 82
Barry, Christy 41, 97
BBC World Service 129
Black and Tans 148, 149
Blessed Well 82
Bloomsbury Set 25, 146, 149
Bog Slide of 1900 24
Bohemians 146
Bothy Band 39
Breathnach, Breandán 70, 71, 73, 84
Breathnach, Seán Bán 96
Brehon 10, 139
Burren 9, 148
Byrnes, Martín 36, 83, 84, 92

C

Cailín Deas Crúite na mBó 33
Caoilte, Jamsie 36, 38, 39, 100
Caoilte, Martin 63
Carey, Johnny (Seán Ó Carún) 121
Carty's Reel 82
Casey, Bobby 72, 79
Celtic Twilight 40
changeling 58

Chelsea Set 146, 149
Clancy, Willie 36, 37, 79, 92, 95
Clannad 86
Clare Champion, The 148
Clarke's tin whistle 75, 109
Cliffs of Moher 9, 63, 96
Cnoc an Chrochaire 10, 140
Coady, Michael 36, 37, 92
Conaola, The Slipper 113
Conlon, Michileen 54, 66, 84
Conlon, The Bazer 66
Connemara 50, 63
Connole, Jerome 66, 77
Connole, Thomas 77
Conway, Ollie 87
Coole Park 144, 150, 151
Cultural tourists 39
Cumann Béaloideas Éireann 51
Curry, Eugene 15
Curtis, PJ 41

D

Dancing teachers 113
Davoran brothers 35, 66, 77
De Danann 39
Delargy, Séamus 28, 32, 43, 51, 90, 121, 122
de Valera 34, 148, 154
Doegan Project 64
Donoghue, 'Styke' 32, 77
Doolin 6, 12, 13
    Doolin Cattle Drive 25, 144
    Doolin Cave 34
    Doolin Céilí Band 92
    Doolin dances 108, 112
    Doolin Ferry 38
    Doolin House 27, 143, 145, 146, 147, 150

Index

Doolin Miners 31
Doolin mines 30, 80, 91
Doolin, population 44
Doolin Storytellers 119
Doolin Wren Boys 114
Doonagore 10, 75
    Doonagore Castle 22, 100, 140
    Doonagore quarry 23
    Doonagore village 23
Doonmacfelim 10
Doran, Johnny 79, 82
draíocht 44
Dromoland Castle 140
Dubliners, The 93
Dylan, Thomas 153

E

Ediphone 121, 124
Ennis, Séamus 32, 35, 36, 66, 70, 81, 90, 91
Ennistymon House 142, 143, 150, 152

F

fairies 56, 57, 58
Falls Hotel 153
Family and Community in Ireland 29
Finucane, Susannah 142
Fisherstreet 9, 14, 40, 48, 49, 50
Fitzgerald, Paddy 67
Flanagans 74
    Flanagan, Kate 69
    Flanagan, Pádraig ('Sober') 54, 66 75, 76, 90, 106
    Flanagan, Peaitsín Mhurty 66, 90, 119, 121
    Flanagan, Tim 37
fleadhs 36, 83
folklore 124
Folklore of Ireland Society 28

Folk Revival/Ballad Boom 37
Fureys, The 86

G

Gaeltacht 51
gambling and dancing 116
Garland Sunday 82
Gentry 137
Gleninagh Castle 142
Glorawn 99
Gore 12, 13, 21, 62
Gregory, Lady 144, 150
Gregory, Robert 143, 148
Griffin, Kevin 41

H

Hardy, Stepheneen 54, 56, 75, 76, 107
Harvard Irish Survey 28
Hayes, P. Joe 72
H.B.H Travel Journal 19
History and Topography of County Clare 13
HMS Hood 155
HMS Magpie 61, 62
Hone, Joseph 154, 155
house dances 78, 81, 100, 116
Howley, Anthony 97
Hynes, Dean, 35, 66, 77
Hynes, Michael 40, 97
Hynes, P.J. 40, 97

I

Inisheer 38, 50, 113
In Our Own Dear Land 26
IRA 27, 149, 150
Ireland: A Nation's Memory 95
Irish Brigade 12, 142

Index

Irish Countryman, The 29
Irish Folk Festival Tour 71, 86
Irish language 9, 28, 50, 51
Irish Tourist Association 30
Irish traditional arts 9

J

John, Augustus 9, 25, 143, 144, 147
Judge Cummins 30

K

Kaul, Adam 43
Kelly, John 72
Kilfenora 108
Killilagh 10
Killilagh Church 16
Killougherys 105-114
    Killoughery, John 104, 106
    Killoughery, Martin 'Tarbert' 35, 77, 106
    Killoughery, Paddy 35, 38, 77, 78, 83, 91, 104, 106, 114
    Killoughery, Paddy 'Tarbert' 66
    Killoughery, Thady 76, 100, 107
Killstuipheen 60, 61, 82, 153
Kimball, Solon T. 29
kitchen middens 9, 21
Knockfinn 12, 13

L

Lá an Baton Charge 25, 145
Lambe, Eugene 41
Leabhar Stiofáin Uí Ealaoire 128, 129, 130, 134
Leyden, Joe 93
Limerick Field Club 21
Liscannor 24
Lisdoonvarna 19, 52
Lisdoonvarna Folk Festival 40

Luogh 24, 28, 52, 74, 89

M

MacClancys 138-142
MacClancy, Boetius 10, 22, 59, 138, 140
MacClancy School of Law and Poetics 13, 138
MacMahon, Tony 37, 84, 85, 95
MacMathúna, Ciarán 35, 36, 83
MacMathúna, Seán 28, 79, 119, 127
MacNamaras 142-155
    MacNamara, Bartholomew 142
    MacNamara, Bridget 152
    MacNamara, Bridgit 146
    MacNamara, Caitlin 146, 151, 152
    MacNamara, Francis 9, 25, 143, 147
    MacNamara, George 148
    MacNamara, Henry Valentine (H.V.) 143
    MacNamara, H.V. 25, 27, 148, 150
    Macnamara, John 155
    MacNamara, John 144, 146
    MacNamara, Major William Nugent 13,
    MacNamara, Nicolette 146, 151, 155
    MacNamara, Pat 155
MacNamara, Stevie 94
MacNeill, Edie 151, 152
Mairnéalach Loinge Mé 33
Majolier, Yvonne 144
Marionettes 146
Mary Anne 151, 152
Mary Poppins 151
McDermott's 35, 36, 41
McGann's 35, 42
McGrath, Mrs. 108
Molloy, Matt 39
Moloney, Annie (Russell) 69
Moloney, Anthony 32, 90, 123

INDEX

Moloney, Mick 85, 87
Moloney's Jig 74
Moloney, The Captain 66, 74, 75
Mrs. McGrath 108
Music Makers 66 -118
Murphy, Gertie 30, 32

N

na Daoine Maithe (fairies) 56
North West Clare 106

O

O'Brien, Bill 38
O'Brien, Cuckoo 32, 50, 81, 146, 148, 152, 155
O'Callaghan, Iris 151, 152, 154
O'Carún, Seán 18, 125, 119, 131
O'Casey, Seán 152
O'Connor, Doll 39
O'Connor, Gus 6, 35, 36
O'Connor, Rory 36, 38, 100
O'Connor's bar 13, 39, 43, 54
O'Connor, Susan 85
O'Donovan, John 15
O'Flaherty, Gerry 38
O'Flaherty, Liam 152
Ó Flanagáin, Peaitsín Mhurty (see Flanagan) 32, 65, 127
Ó hAllmhuráin, Gearóid 44
O'Neill, Eoin 43
Ordnance Survey Letters, Killiliagh 15
overlooked 56

P

People, Place and Culture 9-44
Peoples, Tommy 39
Perrott, Sir John 138

Piggott, Charlie 73
Piper's Chair 72, 77, 81 (tune)
Plain Set 113
poitín 36, 50, 101, 153
Pol an Ionain 34
Poor Little Fisherboy 86
potholers 34
Public Dance Halls Act 116

R

Radio Éireann 83, 91
Rineen Ambush 149
Roadford 14, 28, 35, 52
Russells Brothers 69-101
    Russell, Annie 66
    Russell, Austin (Aughty) 66, 69, 74
    Russell, Austin Rúa 69
    Russell, Gussie 38, 69, 80, 97
    Russell, Micho 26, 35, 37, 38, 40, 69, 71, 112
    Russell, Pakie 6, 27, 32, 35, 36, 69, 79, 80, 89, 108, 117
    Russell Weekend 44
Ryan, Joe 72

S

San Francisco Celtic Music & Arts Festival 73
Sarsfield, Catherine 142
Sarsfield, John 10
Schools' Manuscript Collection 29
Scrap Parties (post-swarie) 115
sean nós singer 69
Set-dancing 112
Shannon, Noreen 13
Shannon, Paddy Pharaic Mhichil 7, 13, 38, 49, 98
Shannon, Willie Beg 39, 54
Shaw, George Bernard 25
Sherlock, Michael 40

Index

Sherlock, Paddy 122
shop ledger 53
sí gaoithe 58, 60
Sinn Féin 148
small mummers (junior Wren Boys) 99
Spanish Armada 10, 59, 139
Stamer, Jane 142
stone axe factory 21
stonemason 89
storytellers 66
Strawboy Dances 112
Strawboys 114, 115
Swaries 112, 114
Sweeney's Men 93

T

Talty, Martin 36, 72, 79, 92, 109
'The Reverend' 143
'The Terror' 143
The Way Were 48-59
Thomond 10
Tír na nÓg 61
Tolkien 9
Toomullin 12, 14
tournaments 116
tradition-bearers 7, 9, 66
Travers, Pamela L 151, 154
Tuath Clae 10
Tuath Clae, Townlands 11
Tuath Clae map 17

U

Uí Ealaoire, Stiofán 18, 28, 123, 131, 144, 145

W

Wagner, Heinrich 51
War of Independence 27, 148
West Clare Railway 19, 145
Westropp, Thomas 21, 22
Willie Clancy Summer School 72
World War II 154
Wren Boys 54
WWI 148

Y

Yeats 68, 144, 148, 150, 151, 152, 153

EDDIE STACK is from Ennistymon, County Clare, Ireland. He learned Irish traditional music from his grandmother, Susan O'Sullivan (Flanagan), and plays mandolin and bouzouki. In his teens he regularly came to the Doolin sessions and played with the Russells, Killougherys and others.

In the late-1980s he moved to San Francisco and co-founded the Irish Arts Foundation with Peter O'Neill. The IAF produced the *San Francisco Celtic Music & Arts Festival* and other cultural events in the 1990s.

Eddie Stack is the author of four collections of short stories, several novellas and a novel. He has received an 'American Small Press Publisher of the Year Award' and a 'Top 100 Irish-American Award' for his fiction. His work has appeared in literary reviews and anthologies internationally, including *Fiction, Confrontation, Whispers & Shouts, Crannog, Southwords* and *Criterion*; *State of the Art: Stories from New Irish Writers*; *Bloomsbury Irish Christmas Stories*, *The Clare Anthology* and *Fiction in the Classroom*. He has recorded spoken word versions of his stories, with music by Martin Hayes and Dennis Cahill. Eddie Stack teaches at UC Berkeley, California.

www.eddiestack.com

Eddie Stack's books are available from all good indie bookstores and may be ordered online from: www.scealeilebooks.ie, www.charliebyrne.com and www.kennys.ie. Print and ebook editions of his books are available at: www.amazon.com/author/eddiestack

SHORT STORIES
The West: Stories from Ireland
Out of the Blue
Quare Hawks
Borderlines*

NOVEL
Heads*

NOVELLAS
The Irish: 3 Novellas*
(The Poet, the Psychic and the Knave;
The Book; Simple Twist of Fate)

* Books available for only Kindle and Kindle apps on iPads. www.amazon.com/author/eddiestack

Free for iPhone & iPad: Time Passes, a prize winning short story by Eddie Stack in print and audio, with art by Phillip Morrison and music by Martin Hayes & Dennis Cahill. Download from iTunes: http://tinyurl.com/lavsvm

"Variously fantastic, comic, elegiac and nostaligic, Mr. Stack's fiction is versatile and engaging...a vivid, compassionate, authentic voice...The West secures him a place in the celebrated tradition of his country's storytelling." —New York Times Book Review

"Eddie Stack would drive you mad with merriment. He would also make you sigh soulfully for the human condition. Put away Jennifer Johnston, William Trevor, Molly Keane and take up The West, a little volume of delights." — Irish Edition

"Eddie Stack's stories jet back and forth across the Atlantic, contrasting small town Ireland and big city US. Every time they land, the author seems to test the borderline of what might and might not be possible in downtown bars, crumbling dance halls and drizzly farms. The result is a remarkably consistent collection of short stories." —Southword

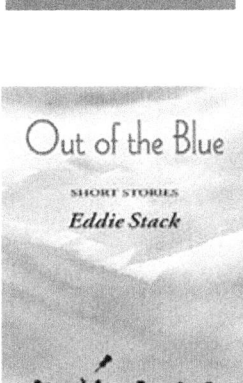

"There's a genuinely wild and fugitive comic sense in Eddie Stack's tales that puts one in mind of Myles na Gopaleen as much as the salt spume dam, George Makay Brown. The fantastical and the everyday combine with wit, sharpness and brio. Never sentimental, often funny, always accurate...this is pithy, finely tuned writing of a high order." —Observer

"Quare Hawks is a collision between old and new Ireland. Both heartbreaking and hilarious, and hopeful and despairing. Eddie Stack has a way of making you laugh and cry at the same time. A brilliant collection from a great Irish storyteller." —Willy Vlautin

"Exceptionally stories—an authentic voice of the migrant Irish." —San Francisco Chronicle

"Haunting stories, filled with beautifully sketched characters. A lively storyteller in a long and hallowed tradition." —Philadelphia Inquirer

Lightning Source UK Ltd.
Milton Keynes UK
UKOW07f1846021116
286720UK00010B/78/P

9 781930 579033